Cumberland County
Facts and Folklore

Cumberland County Facts and Folklore

Laurie Glenn Norris

NIMBUS
PUBLISHING

Dedicated to my grandparents:

Sherman Charles Glenn

Sarah Elizabeth (Cormier) Glenn

Irving Alexander (Sandy) Smith

Mabel Mary (Bourgeois) Smith

They lived their lives here.

Nimbus Publishing Limited
PO Box 9166, Halifax, NS, B3K 5M8
(902) 455-4286, www.nimbus.ca

Printed and bound in Canada
Cover illustration: Mike Holmes
Design: Matt Reid
Author photo: Laura Ritchie

Library and Archives Canada Cataloguing in Publication

Glenn Norris, Laurie, 1957-
Cumberland County : facts and folklore / Laurie Glenn Norris.
Includes bibliographical references.
ISBN 978-1-55109-731-2

1. Cumberland (N.S. : County)—History. 2. Cumberland (N.S. : County)—Miscellanea. I. Title.

FC2345.C84N67 2009 971.6'11 C2009-903370-4

Canada

The Canada Council for the Arts | Le Conseil des Arts du Canada

NOVA SCOTIA
Tourism, Culture and Heritage

We acknowledge the financial support of the Government of Canada through the Book Publishing Industry Development Program (BPIDP) and the Canada Council, and of the Province of Nova Scotia through the Department of Tourism, Culture and Heritage for our publishing activities.

This book was printed on Ancient-Forest Friendly paper

ANCIENT FOREST FRIENDLY™

Table of Contents

Acknowledgements

Thank you to the following individuals for providing information and good ideas: Ken Adams, Patricia Lee Belier, Adri Boodoosingh, Diana Boodoosingh, Jenna Boon, Elaine Bourque, Kay Brown, Alec Burbine, Sherry Burbine, Beatrice Burgess, Avis Chapman, Susan Clarke, Leta Clayden, Trudy Clinton, Darrell Cole, Dave Copus, Ken Crowley, Laurie Crowley, Dave Dewar, Bronwyn Foreward, Gordon Glennie, Mary Hastings, Glenda Janes, Judy Jollymore, Karen Jost, Rena Kossatz, Gary Landry, John Leroux, Mary Mackinnon, Bill McAloney, Wilfred Morris, Anne Newman, Oralee O'Byrne, Councillor John Reid, Mayor Doug Robinson, Helen Sims, Jim Talbot, Laurene Thompson, Marie-Paule Thorn, Andrew Wagstaff, Sarah Welton, and Linda Wooliever.

Special thanks go to: Robin Sutherland, for suggesting I send my list of Cumberland County phrases to a publisher for consideration; Amherst historian John MacKay, for generously sharing his research with me; Shirley Nickerson and her staff at the Cumberland County Museum and Archives, for their cheerful willingness to fulfil my every request; Rachelle Goguen, Jesse Marchand, Kelsey McLaren, and Patrick Murphy at Nimbus Publishing, for taking a chance on a first-time author; my sister, Maureen Glennie, and best friend, Barb Thompson, who are my research soul mates; my parents, Reg and Annie Glenn, for sharing their memories with me through the years, and Mum for her great detective skills; and my husband and sweetheart, Barry Norris, whose love and support made this book possible.

Cumberland County Facts and Folklore does little more than scratch the surface of all the interesting things that could be written about Cumberland County. Any errors and omissions here are entirely my own.

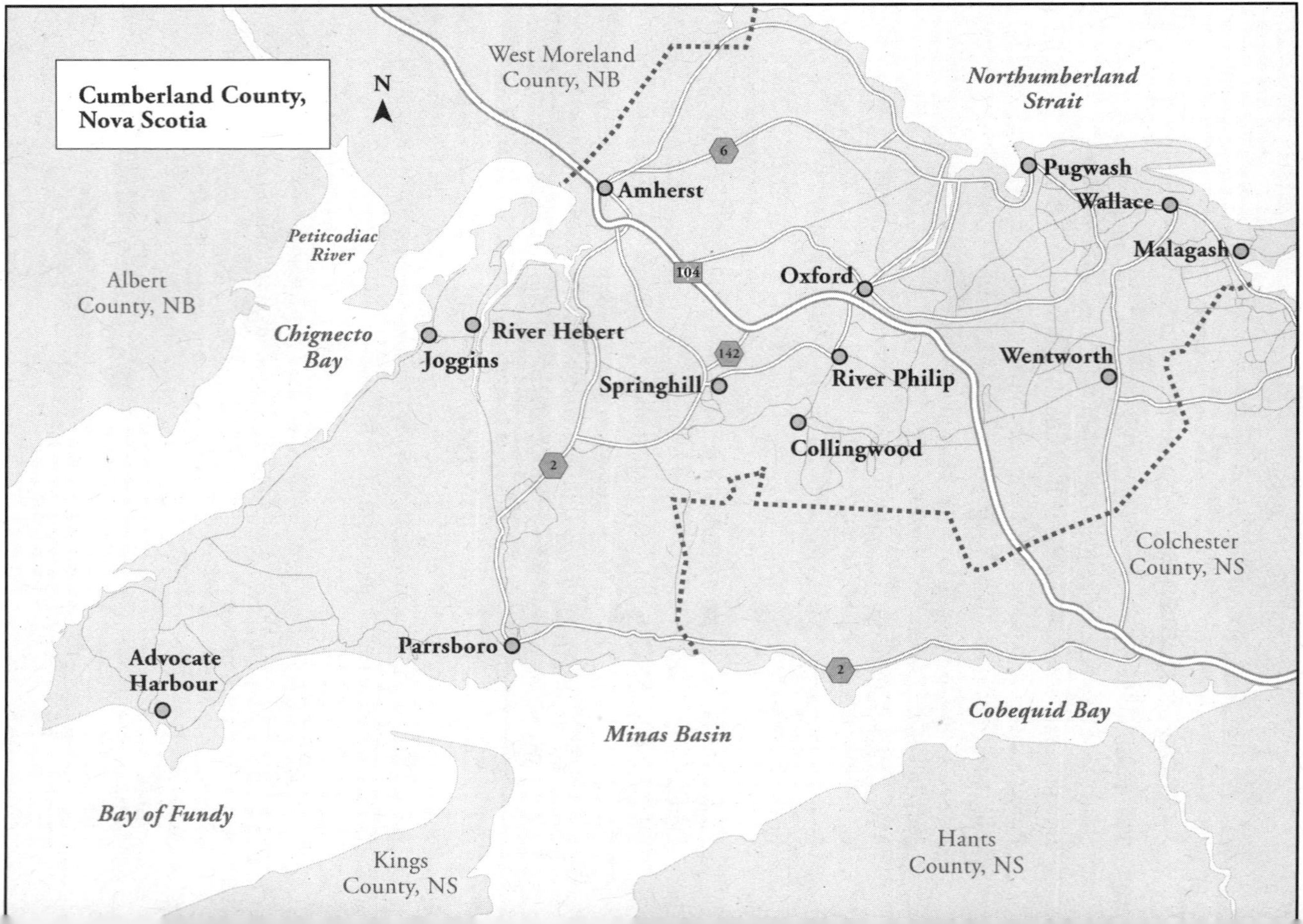
Cumberland County,
Nova Scotia
N
West Moreland
County, NB
Northumberland
Strait
6
Pugwash
Amherst
Wallace
Petitcodiac
River
Malagash
Albert
County, NB
104
Oxford
Chignecto
Bay
River Hebert
Joggins
142
Wentworth
Springhill
River Philip
Collingwood
2
Colchester
County, NS
Parrsboro
Advocate
Harbour
2
Cobequid Bay
Minas Basin
Bay of Fundy
Hants
County, NS
Kings
County, NS

Where My World Began

In her 1976 essay "Where the World Began," about her hometown of Manawaka, Manitoba, Margaret Laurence examines what makes her community unique and what similarities tie it to other communities around the globe. But, as Laurence writes, part of Manawaka's history is lost, since the place is "inhabited by the unknowable dead, [which] includes ancestors—both [her] own and other people's."

In Cumberland County, where my world began, ancestors are knowable, unlike those in Manawaka. They become known and remain known through the stories we hear and continue to tell. Ever since I was a child I've heard parents and grandparents and friends tell stories about the county, about its people, past and present—those who were born here, who lived here, or who were just passing through. There are stories about farming, fishing, and mining, about accomplishments, failures, natural disasters, and world wars, stories about hard times and funny times. Quarrels, hopes, triumphs, and tragedies—all have played out in Cumberland County. The wrongs and slights of decades (sometimes of centuries) past are remembered and related. They are told in the county's own unique words and voices. Passing these stories on to the next generation then becomes both our responsibility and our delight.

I am privileged in *Cumberland County Facts and Folklore* to make a contribution to this handing down of our county's stories, its interesting tidbits, its unique aspects. Where my world began has some of the most ancient fossils, most plentiful and delicious blueberries, and highest tides. Like all other places, however, Cumberland County has seen its tragedies—its young men lost in war or in dangerous coal mines. It has struggled with poverty, unemployment, and out-migration. And yet Cumberland County survives and thrives. Just as the county's unique geography binds Nova Scotia to the continent so its unique culture and history, like that of Laurence's Manawaka, bind it to the experience of the rest of the world.

Whether Cumberland County or some faraway land is where your world began, you will find things here that are new and things that remind you of home. And there are still so many stories to tell, so many ancestors to know.

Laurie Glenn Norris
April 2009

Places

Just the Facts Ma'am

Cumberland County was created by order of the Governor and Council of the colony of Nova Scotia on August 17, 1759.

Cumberland, along with Annapolis, Kings, and Lunenburg counties, was originally part of Halifax County. At the time the area that is now New Brunswick was part of the colony of Nova Scotia and was included within the jurisdiction of Cumberland County.

When Parrsboro Township (originally in Kings County) was divided in 1840, part of it was annexed by Cumberland County and the rest of it went to Colchester County.

The county's name is derived from Fort Cumberland, which is what the British renamed Fort Beauséjour after its capture in 1755. Both the fort and the county were named for the Duke of Cumberland, Prince William Augustus (1721–1765), by General Robert Monckton, who led the British forces in their defeat of the French at Fort Beauséjour and became the lieutenant-governor of Nova Scotia that same year. Cumberland had been the captain general of the British army and Monckton's patron. He was nicknamed "Butcher of Cumberland" for his treatment of the Jacobites at the 1746 Battle of Culloden. The noxious weed "Stinking Willie" was also named for him. A fort, a county, and a weed—go figure.

The crest of the Cumberland County Municipality Corporation—a shaft of yellow wheat on a background of blue sky and brown earth—pays tribute to the county's long and prosperous agricultural history.

The motto of the Cumberland County Municipality Corporation: To provide residents with leadership, support, and municipal services that contribute to the well-being of the community.

* Population: 32,046
* Female: 16,535 Male: 15,515

Source: StatsCan 2006

We're Bigger

Cumberland County is the 4th largest county in Nova Scotia. Totalling 4,200 square kilometres, it's just a bit bigger than the old northern English county of Cumberland (3,926 sq. km); Long Island, New York (3,643 sq. km); and the state of Rhode Island (3,156 sq. km).

Where Are We?

Cumberland County is located:

* at 45–46 degrees north latitude (same as Milan, Italy) and 63–65 degrees west longitude (same as the Virgin Islands).
* at an average elevation of 5.56 metres (18.25 feet) above sea level.

Did you know...

...that some of the rocks in Cumberland County are among the oldest on Earth?

High Land

Cape Chignecto, a headland located on the Bay of Fundy in Cumberland County, contains the highest cliffs on the Nova Scotia peninsula.

And So It Goes

About 600 million years ago, present-day Cumberland County was linked with what is now northern Europe.

Now That's Old!

During the Upper Carboniferous Period (310–290 million years ago), most of present-day Cumberland County was covered with lush vegetation and swamps. Plants would die in these swamps, and, after many years, become compressed and form thick layers of peat. In time, this organic matter would turn to coal. The large trees that covered the area were inhabited by amphibians, reptiles, and insects, which would also become compressed and fossilized, along with the plant matter. The Joggins Fossil Cliffs contain some of the world's oldest fossils.

The Parrsboro area of the Bay of Fundy is home to 200-million-year-old dinosaur bones.

Baby, It Was Cold Outside!

The last ice age ended about 12,000 years ago. Before that time Cumberland County, along with most of the rest of what would become Canada, was covered with several hundred metres of glacial ice. The glaciers began to melt, and disappeared about 7,000 years ago. These glaciers and their movement over land had a profound effect upon the geology and landscape of Cumberland County.

Largest in Cumberland County / Largest in North America

In 1984 researchers discovered 100,000 pieces of fossilized reptile bones along the Bay of Fundy coast near Parrsboro. It was the largest discovery of vertebrate fossils ever made in North America.

From the Beginning

During the area's prehistory, the Mi'kmaq controlled land from the St. Croix River, Piziquid (present-day Hants County) and Cobequid (present-day Colchester County), to Chignecto (containing present-day Cumberland County), which was their principal settlement.

From the time of first contact, the French relied on Mi'kmaq guides to help them explore the area. The Mi'kmaq passed along their names for landmarks and waterways. These names stuck, and soon began appearing in written records and on charts. The Mi'kmaq were good geographers, and used landmarks and distinguishing features as place names, many of which are still used today.

The Mi'kmaq subdivided the present-day Maritime provinces into eight distinct districts. One of these was Siknikt, whose boundaries included present-day Albert and Westmorland counties in New Brunswick, and Cumberland County in Nova Scotia.

The Mi'kmaq called the area that is now Cumberland County *Kwesomalegak*, which means "hardwood point."

The word *Siknikt* (meaning "great marsh area") was later corrupted into Chignecto by the French explorers. The first land grant for the county of Chignecto was dated October 24, 1676, and given by Comte de Frontenac, governor of Canada, to Michel Leneuf de La Vallière. This grant is believed to have included "the land between the rivers River Philip and Shemogue, extending back...on the Petitcodiac to near Springhill in Cumberland."

Don't Miss the Isthmus

The *Oxford English Reference Dictionary* defines an isthmus as "a narrow piece of land connecting two larger pieces of land."

At its narrowest point the Isthmus of Chignecto is 24 kilometres wide.

The Isthmus of Siknikt (Chignecto) played a major role in the history of the founding of North America and the fight for its possession amongst the native peoples, the French, and the English.

The central location and geography of the isthmus made it a point of convergence for several important transportation, portage, and communication routes; it was accessible from the peninsula of Nova Scotia and from what was to become New Brunswick, Prince Edward Island, and Cape Breton. For the Mi'kmaq it was a wintering place for shelter and hunting. During the period of French dominance in the area, it was a communications link between New France and Acadia. After the 1759 British conquest, the isthmus continued to be used until the first road linking the Memramcook Valley with the Tantramar Marshes was constructed. The first intercolonial railroad closely mimicked the location of the old isthmus portage route.

The British raised the stakes in the fight for North America in 1750 by constructing Fort Lawrence on the ruins of the Acadian village of Beaubassin. The French retaliated with the building of Fort Beauséjour. The two forts faced each other across the Missiguash River. Military historian Chris Hand contends that "the situation on the Chignecto Isthmus was without parallel in the whole of North America. It was the only location where French and British forces were close enough to see each other and to have direct contact."

The British captured Fort Beauséjour in 1755 and renamed it Fort Cumberland. It continued to play a key role in the fortunes of North America during the American Revolution when it again saw combat. It remained a military fort until 1833.

Did you know...

...that the British siege of Fort Beauséjour in 1755 marked the first shots fired in the Seven Years War (1756–1763), which led to the fall of the French Empire in North America?

...that until 1765 Fort Beauséjour was part of Cumberland County? Now it is in Westmorland County, New Brunswick.

Splish Splash

Bay of Fundy

The name, Bay of Fundy, is believed to have been coined by Portuguese sailors in the sixteenth century, who called it *rio fundo*, meaning "deep river." The Bay of Fundy is encased in a 200-million-year-old rift valley. It is funnel-shaped, with its width varying from 120 kilometres at Yarmouth to 45 kilometres at Cape Chignecto. The upper part of the bay splits into Chignecto Bay in the northeast and the Minas Basin in the east. The Bay of Fundy is noted for its red mud.

Chignecto Bay

Chignecto Bay is an inlet of the Bay of Fundy that branches to the northeast between New Brunswick and Nova Scotia and divides into the Shepody Bay and the Cumberland Basin.

Cumberland Basin

Cumberland Basin is the northeast arm of Chignecto Bay. The basin flows into the Bay of Fundy between Fort Lawrence and Cape Chignecto. It ends at the Tantramar Marshes and the estuaries of the Tantramar and Maccan rivers. The French called it Beaubassin, meaning beautiful basin; the English gave it the name that it bears today.

Neville Lake

Neville Lake is a glacial lake in the centre of the county. Its surface elevation is 18 metres above sea level.

Northumberland Strait

The Northumberland Strait is situated in the southern part of the Gulf of St. Lawrence. It is home to some of the warmest ocean water temperatures on the Atlantic coast north of Virginia.

West Bay

West Bay is a small bay along the Minas Basin, situated to the west of Partridge Island.

Rivers

- During the 1700s, the Missiquash River was the boundary between French and English territory in what is today Cumberland County. Its name comes from the Mi'kmaq word meaning "marsh river."
- The Maccan River is a tidal river. Nappan River is one of its tributaries, as are Kennedy Creek, Patton Creek, and St. George's Brook.
- Tidal bores can be seen from both the Maccan Tidal View Wetland Park and from the Tidal Bore Park in River Hebert. A tidal bore is the leading edge of an incoming tide that forms a wave which travels against the current. Bores often occur in areas where there is a wide range between high and low tides—something for which the Bay of Fundy is famous.
- Farrell River flows from MacAloney's Lake into Parrsboro Harbour on the Minas Basin.
- Ward's Falls, near Wharton, is situated along the migratory path of the monarch butterfly.

Did you know...

...that Partridge Island has been a peninsula since the 1869 Saxby Gale? The force of the winds and water during the storm formed a sandbar isthmus that connected it to the mainland.

Islands in the Sun

Isle Haute

Isle Haute is located at the entrance to Minas Basin and can be seen from Advocate Harbour. The explorer Samuel de Champlain gave it its name due to its height.

Tonge Island

Tonge Island was first called Île de la Vallerie. In May 1760 British engineer Winckworth Tonge was given the grant for the island. It continued to be privately owned well into the 1900s.

The Land We Live On

Must Have Semi-Precious!

Agate and amethyst can be found along the beaches of the Parrsboro Shore.

Mountain High...Valley Low

The Cobequid Mountains rise to 300 metres and extend for 120 kilometres across Cumberland County. They are in the Maritime Acadian Highlands, part of the Appalachian Mountain Range that was formed over many millions of years—up until the Devonian Period (417–354 million years ago). The mountains are composed of granite and volcanic rocks, all of which have been crushed and folded by continental drift.

The Wentworth Valley is a glacial trough north of Folly Mountain and is the lowest elevation pass through the Cobequid Mountains. It is also the shortest route between Halifax and the New Brunswick border.

Ever the Pest

Mi'kmaq taught the early European arrivals to smear bear grease on their bodies to keep away mosquitoes and blackflies.

One immigrant to Cumberland County in the 1770s observed: "Everyone in this country wears trousers, and some of the women wear them, for the mosquitoes fly up their petticoats and bite them terribly!"

Did you know...

... that prior to August 1996 the only two documented sites for the long-tailed upland shrew (the *Sorex dispar*) in Nova Scotia were along the Wentworth Valley?

Up a Tree

Originally, most of Cumberland County was covered with trees. Today it contains no virgin forests.

Weather, Weather Everywhere

- During the 1700s, Yorkshire settlers described the bitter spring rains on the Isthmus of Chignecto as "sheep killers."
- On February 18, 1922, a record low temperature of -37.2 degrees Celsius was recorded in Cumberland.
- On August 16, 1954, a record high temperature of 34.4 degrees Celsius was recorded.
- Extreme daily rainfall: September 22, 1942, 153.7 mm
- Extreme daily snowfall: April 8, 1963, 40.6 cm

Hit the Road

Before the 1790s, roads in Cumberland County were little more than paths; most of them were old trails created by the Mi'kmaq. Winter was the best season of travel as the cold weather froze lakes and rivers.

Nathaniel Smith wrote home to England on August 15, 1775, about travelling by horse and sleigh: "we can run over undyked marshes and rivers to any place we want. If we ride to a neighbour's House at Fort Lawrence or Cumberland, you will meet perhaps four, five, or more Slays driving away with all fury…"

The coach road that ran from Halifax to the "fort near Amherst" was known as "The Great Northern Road." In 1829 it took 52 hours for a two-horse coach to travel between Halifax and Amherst. The Wentworth Valley and River Philip were important stops along the way. In 1836 coach service between Amherst and Saint John was established.

On November 11, 1872, the first train reached Amherst and the days of the coach were over.

Keep on Truckin'

As of 2008, there were 1,205 kilometres of paved road and 617 kilometres of gravel road in Cumberland County.

Country Roads

During the eighteenth and nineteenth centuries, the usual route from Amherst to Windsor or Halifax was by way of a narrow eight-mile ridge called the Boar's Back Road. This road was formed by glaciers moving over the area, shoving rocks and debris ahead of it. It was narrow and rough—like the top of a boar's back—hence its name.

The Glooscap Trail hugs the Minas Basin shore and connects Wolfville, in Kings County, with Amherst.

The Sunrise Trail is located on the north shore of the Northumberland Strait. It is 316 km (196 miles) long and stretches from Amherst to the Canso Causeway.

Did you know...

...that there are 274 bridges in Cumberland County?

Townships

In 1759 the Township of Cumberland was created. It was 100,000 acres in size and included the Fort Cumberland and Fort Lawrence Ridges. It extended west to the River Aulac, eastward to the River La Planche, and northeast to Baie Verte and was bounded on the southwest by the Cumberland Basin.

In 1763 the townships of Sackville and Amherst were created. Sackville Township included the lands west of the River Aulac and the Tantramar Marsh. Amherst Township extended roughly from present-day Amherst Point to present-day Amherst Head.

Today Cumberland County consists of 5 municipalities: the towns of Amherst, Oxford, Parrsboro, and Springhill, and the municipality of Cumberland, which is the remainder of the county and its incorporated villages.

Communities

Many of the names of Cumberland's towns and villages originated from Mi'kmaq words, from the names of British officers, or for the communities left behind by homesick settlers. Many of Cumberland's place names became formalized by the 1864 Nova Scotia School Act, when it became necessary to form demarcated school sections. The formation of post offices also led to a greater need for place names to have designated boundaries.

Advocate Harbour

One of the oldest villages in Atlantic Canada and one of the oldest place names on the Minas Basin. It is included on a 1685 map, where it is called Havre à l'Avocat.

Low tide at Advocate Harbour

Amherst

The shiretown and largest community in the county, and also the geographical centre of the Maritimes. The Mi'kmaq called the area *Nemcheboogwek*, meaning "going up rising ground," and used it as a spring camp in order to hunt the birds that came to the marsh. The Acadians called it *Les Planches*, referring to the planks or boards laid down between it and the Tantramar Marsh. In 1764 it was renamed Amherst in recognition of Lord Jeffrey Amherst (1717–1797), who was appointed commander-in-chief of the British forces in North America in 1758. Current population: 9,505.

Amherst Shore

Originally called Rockwell Settlement.

Apple River

Originally called *Agoomakun*, meaning "herring fishery."

Athol

Originally called Little Forks.

Brookdale

Its first name was River Nappan—named for the river that runs through the village.

Did you know...

...that the community of Athol is the boundary, or school line, and establishes whether students, according to the location of their home, attend Parrsboro Regional High School or River Hebert District High School?

Cape d'Or

Located at the entrance to Minas Basin. Copper was discovered in the area in the early 1600s and was mistaken for gold—hence the name.

Dramatic view of the Bay of Fundy at Cape d'Or

Collingwood

Named for Admiral Lord Collingwood, second-in-command to Lord Nelson at Trafalgar.

Conn Mills

Named for an early settler who was a mill owner.

Diligent River

Named in 1785 by Governor John Parr who was impressed with the "diligence" of its Loyalist settlers.

Fenwick

Named for Sir Fenwick Williams, lieutenant-governor of Nova Scotia from 1865–1867.

Hastings

Originally known as Porter Town. The name was changed in 1864, likely in honour of Warren Hastings (1732–1818), the first governor-general of India.

Joggins

Located at the head of the Bay of Fundy. Its name is derived from the Mi'kmaq word *chegoggin*, which means "a place of fish weirs." It was included on maps as early as 1750. In 1851 Sir Charles Lyell and Sir William Dawson discovered terrestrial reptiles within fossilized trees in Joggins.

Leamington

Originally known as the Maccan Mountain.

Leicester

Named for an English city of the same name. Over time, the pronunciation of the name has changed from "lester" to "lie-cester."

Linden

Originally known as Goose River; in 1882 it was named for the Linden tree.

Lorneville

Received its present name in 1878 when locals petitioned the federal government for a post office.

Lower Cove

Likely named for its geographical location in respect to Minudie.

Maccan

Its name is traceable to the Mi'kmaq word *maakan*, meaning "fishing place."

Malagash

Located on the northwest corner of the county. Its first name was *Malegaawach*, meaning "place of games." Mi'kmaq from the Cobequid Mountains would travel to Malegaawach during the summer months to meet others for games and celebrations.

Mapleton

Located in the centre of the county. It takes its name from the abundance of maple trees in the area. Originally known as Maccan Mountain.

Minudie

The village began as an Acadian settlement called Menoudie, from the Mi'kmaq *munoode*, meaning "sack or bag."

Nappan

Its name is traceable to the Mi'kmaq word *nepan*, thought to mean "a good place to obtain camp or wigwam poles."

Oxford

Thought to have gotten its name due to its location. Those travelling to River Philip would use the settlement as a place to let their oxen ford the river. It once was nicknamed Slabtown owing to its many sawmills and the abundance of slab-wood in the area. It was incorporated as a town in May 1904. Today it's the blueberry capital of the world. Current population: 1,178.

Did you know...

...that Oxford is located at the confluence of three rivers: Black River, River Philip, and Little River?

Oxford Junction

Once known as Clifton.

Parrsboro

The largest community along the north shore of the Minas Basin. Its original name was *Awokun*, meaning "a portage." Later known as Mill Village, it was renamed Parrsboro in honour of Loyalist Governor John Parr (1725–1791). Current population: 1,401.

Port Howe

Likely named in honour of Joseph Howe (1804–1873), who served as MLA for the county from 1851 to 1855. Howe was later premier and lieutenant-governor of Nova Scotia.

Pugwash

Derived from the Mi'kmaq word *pagweak*, meaning "shallow water or shoal." During the 1800s there was a failed attempt to change this "uncouth name" to Waterford.

River Hebert

Named for Louis Hébert (c.1575–1627), an apothecary who travelled from France with Pierre du Gua de Monts, the founder of Port Royal. Hébert is believed to have been part of an exploratory expedition up the river that now bears his name, the pronunciation of which has been anglicized as "Hibbert."

Salem

Originally called Sugarwoods Hill. An important stopping place during stagecoach days.

Shinimicas Bridge

Takes its name from the nearby river, which drains into the Northumberland Strait. Derived from a Mi'kmaq word meaning "shining waters."

Spencer's Island

Located on the north shore of the Minas Basin and named for George Spencer (1758–1834), First Lord of the Admiralty. The area was famous for shipbuilding. The brigantine *Amazon*, which was later renamed the *Mary Celeste*, was built there in 1860.

Springhill

The name is descriptive. The town sits on a hill that once contained many springs. It was once the location of the deepest coal mine in North America. It was incorporated as a town in 1889. Current population: 3,941.

Tidnish

Its name is derived from the Mi'kmaq word *mtagunich*, meaning "paddle."

Truemanville

Named for the Trueman family, one of the first families to settle the area and among the many Yorkshire immigrants to the county in the 1770s.

Wallace

Likely named for Michael Wallace (1747–1831), a provincial treasurer of Nova Scotia. Its original name was Remsheg. May also have been named for William Wallace, Scotland's national hero.

Warren

Named in 1864 for Warren Hastings, first governor-general of India.

Wentworth

Named for Sir John Wentworth (1737–1820), lieutenant-governor of Nova Scotia from 1792 to 1808.

Westchester

Named by Loyalists in 1784 for Westchester County, New York.

Did you know...

...that East Leicester is the only community in Cumberland County originally settled by Black Loyalists, who arrived in the late 1700s?

Communities that Are No More

* Beaubassin was a French settlement on the Isthmus of Chignecto. It had the misfortune to be on the English side of the Missiquash River boundary. The French burned Beaubassin so the Acadians would have to relocate to Fort Beauséjour, on the French side of the river. The village was never rebuilt. Fort Lawrence was constructed near the ruins of the village.
* Eatonville Harbour is now the home of Cape Chignecto's Day-Use Park.
* Shulie, from the French for "shoe" (*soulier*), was once the location of a thriving lumbering community. Today, there are hunting camps in the area.

Environmentally Yours

The Cape Chignecto Provincial Park Phase II consists of a day-use park. It is approximately 20 kilometres from the conventional electrical grid. The Three Sisters Interpretive Centre, situated in the park, is a 1,600-square-foot building powered by a series of solar panels.

The Joggins Fossil Centre is one of the greenest buildings in Atlantic Canada. It has a 50-kilowatt generator, a solar heating system, harvested rainwater, and a green roof.

Springhill's abandoned mines are now used as a unique source of environmentally friendly geothermal energy. The town's community centre is a world-leading example of geothermal energy use.

Did you know...

... that the Amherst Shore Provincial Park is the only place in Nova Scotia where triploid blue-spotted salamanders have been found?

How Many Have You Seen?

In Cumberland County, there are 22 Fundy Shore Ecotour sites:

Advocate Beach
Age of Sail Heritage Centre, Ward's Brook
Amherst Point Migratory Bird Park
AWEsome Park, Nappan
Cape Chignecto Provincial Park
Cape d'Or, Advocate
Fox Point Lookoff
First Beach Interpretive Site, Parrsboro
Fundy Geological Museum, Parrsboro
Heritage Models Centre, River Hebert
Joggins Fossil Centre
Joggins Fossil Cliffs
Maccan Tidal Bore Viewing Area
Minudie Interpretive Park
Nova Scotia Visitor Information Centre, Fort Lawrence
Partridge Island Interpretive Site, Parrsboro
Partridge Island Hiking and Lookoff, Parrsboro
Port Greville Lookoff
River Hebert Tidal Bore Park
Spencer's Island Historic Site
Two Islands Interpretive Site, Parrsboro
Wards Falls Hiking Trails, Wharton

Cumberland County's Provincial Parks

Fox Harbour Provincial Park
Gulf Shore Provincial Park
Heather Beach Provincial Park
Northport Beach Provincial Park
Wentworth Provincial Park
Tidnish Bridge Provincial Park
Tidnish Dock Provincial Park

For Our Fine Feathered Friends

There are 15,000 acres of Ducks Unlimited land in Cumberland County.

Amherst Point Migratory Bird Sanctuary, 429 hectares of safe haven for birds and wildlife, is part of the Chignecto National Wildlife Area. It is the most productive wetland in Nova Scotia and centrally located on the Atlantic Migratory Flyway. Its diverse habitat ensures a variety of birds. In all, 228 species have been sighted in the sanctuary, which became officially protected in 1973. Because its soil contains gypsum, limestone, and marine silt, it has the highest plant productivity of any wetland in Atlantic Canada.

Did you know...

... that you are more likely to see the snowy egret at the Amherst Point Migratory Bird Sanctuary than at any other place in Nova Scotia?

Marsh-Mellow

Tantramar Marsh

The Tantramar Marsh covers over 50,000 hectares (123,500 acres) of tidal waterways, grassy wetlands, and low farmlands recovered from the marsh by the Acadians during the 1700s. It is an important breeding site for over 100 species of birds and is a major annual stopover for hundreds of thousands of migrating birds. It penetrates inland from the Bay of Fundy for 10 kilometres.

Hay from the marsh was shipped for commercial sale along the eastern seaboard and to Europe as late as the 1930s. The hay of the marsh is rich in iodine.

Described as the world's largest hayfield, it once contained over 400 salt-hay storage barns.

First for Cumberland County First for Canada

The John Lusby Marsh, part of the Amherst Point Migratory Bird Sanctuary, was the first area acquired by the Canadian Wildlife Service Program to protect important wetlands in Canada. It is the largest remaining salt marsh in the Bay of Fundy and an important waterfowl staging ground. In the 1960s up to 15,000 Canadian geese stopped there on their flights north and south.

Minudie Marsh

This large marsh situated on the head of the Bay of Fundy was called le champs élysées by the early French explorers. It contains 1,200 hectares of dyked salt marsh and farmland that is leased to the Minudie Pasture Co-op Limited as a community livestock pasture and hay land. It is home to many nesting birds, including ducks, pheasants, short-eared owls, and songbirds.

Be Careful Out There

In Cumberland County there are 6 species at risk, including: 2 birds, 1 reptile, 1 mammal, 1 fish, and 1 lichen. They are:

Piping Plover (*Charadrius melodius*)

Peregrine Falcon (*Falco peregrinus anatum*)

Wood Turtle (*Clemmys insculpta*)

Moose (mainland population) (*Alces americana*)

Atlantic Salmon (inner Bay of Fundy population) (*Salmo salar*)

Boreal Felt Lichen (*Erioderma pendiculata*)

Our Built Heritage is recognized...

...by the municipality...

According to the official Municipality of Cumberland County website, there are 22 municipally registered heritage properties in the county:

Advocate Harbour: Advocate Harbour United Church

Amherst Point: Amherst Point United Church; Forrest/Russell House

Fort Lawrence: John Smith House

Gulf Shore: Melville United Church

Linden: Renwick United Church

Little River: Riverside Farm (built about 1830)

Minudie: Gilbert Seaman House

Pugwash: Pugwash Train Station (built 1888)

River Hebert: Grand Marr Farm (built about 1905)

River Philip: Oxley Homestead; River Philip United Church

Rockley: MacLeod House

Southampton: Lorne Smith House

Spencer's Island: Spencer's Island Lighthouse; Spencer's Island Union Church

Tidnish: Church of the Good Shepherd; Ketchum Cottage

Truemanville: Trueman House

Wallace: Wallace and Area Museum-Davison-Kennedy House (built 1839)

Wentworth: Wentworth Baptist Church

West Advocate: Hill Top Farm

...by the province...

From the Nova Scotia Registry of Historic Places in Cumberland County:

Amherst

The Bank of Montreal Building, 100 Victoria St. (built 1904)

Bank of Nova Scotia, 79 Victoria St. East (built 1907)

Christ Church, 60 Victoria St. East (built 1846)

County Courthouse, 54 Victoria St. East (built 1888)

Cumberland County Museum, Grove Cottage, 150 Church St. (built 1838)

Elmwood House, 233 Victoria St. East (built about 1845)

First Baptist Church, 66 Victoria St. East (built 1895)

Hewson House, 177 Victoria St. East (built 1907)

Lusby House, 46 Victoria St. (built about 1884)

Moss Jewellers Building, 91 Victoria St. East (built 1897)

Old Post Office and Customs Building, 50 Victoria St. East (built 1886)

Trinity St. Stephen's United Church, 1 Ratchford St. (built 1906)

West Highlands School, 30 Hickman St. (built about 1911)

Diligent River

Cannon House, 10215 No. 209 Highway (built about 1808)

Fort Lawrence

Chignecto Ship Railway Terminus, Fort Lawrence Rd. Route 4 (built 1888–1891)

Lower Gulf Shore

Stone House, Gulf Shore Road (built 1833)

Minudie

Amos Thomas Seaman House, Barronsfield Rd. (built 1843)

Minudie School Museum, 5518 Barronsfield Rd. (built 1847)

Minudie United Church of Canada or Universalist Church, 5508 Barronsfield Rd. (built about 1848)

St. Denis Church, 5534 Barronsfield Rd. (built 1848)

North Wallace

Mullins Point Upper Range Lighthouse, North Wallace Rd. (built 1894)

Parrsboro

Civic Building, 4030 Eastern Ave. (built about 1858)

Manning Block, 151 Main St. (built about 1856)

Old Post Office, 168 Main St. (built about 1912)

Ottawa House By-the-Sea, 1155 Whitehall Rd. (built about 1770)

St. George's Anglican Church, 216 Main St. (built about 1865)

Springhill

Lamp Cabin Building, 31 Industrial Park Dr. (built about 1901–1902)

Tidnish Bridge

Tidnish (Keystone) Bridge, Route 366 (built 1888–1891)

Tidnish

Tidnish Dock Site, Route 366 at Tidnish Cross Roads (built 1888–1891)

Wallace

St. Matthew's Presbyterian Church, 3863 No. 307 Hwy (built 1828)

Wallace River

Wallace River Railway Swing Bridge, Route 6 (built about 1889)

...and by the country...

National Historic Sites in Cumberland County:

Beaubassin (Fort Lawrence)

Chapman House (Fort Lawrence)

Fort Lawrence (Fort Lawrence)

Springhill Coal Mining (Springhill)

Murals, Murals, Everywhere Murals

The Amherst Mural Project consists of 11 murals. Can you find them all?

Building the Aboiteau, Victoria Street

Cumberland County Association 25th Anniversary, Acadian Street

Great Amherst Mystery, Havelock Street

History of Education, Prince Arthur Street

History of Transportation, Station Street

Hockey Heritage, Amherst Stadium

Mansour's Mural, corner of Church and Electric Streets

Music Mural, Princess Street

North Nova Scotia Highlanders, corner of Havelock and Ratchford streets

Old Home Week 1910, corner of Havelock and Victoria streets

Women's Mural, Prince Arthur Street

Happy Trails to You

Some of the Cumberland County trails included in the Nova Scotia Trails Federation Fundy Region Trails are:

- Amherst Point Migratory Bird Sanctuary Trail, owned by the Canadian Wildlife Service, Environment Canada (2.5 km).
- Amherst Shore Provincial Park Trail, owned by the Province of Nova Scotia (4 km). The park's main hiking trail is 2.5 km long.
- Ketchum Trail, located on Route 366 in Tidnish (3.7 km).
- Partridge Island Trail, owned privately (2.7 km).
- Tidnish Dock Provincial Park, maintained by the Nova Scotia Department of Natural Resources (500 m).
- Wallace Bay National Wildlife Area Trail, owned by the Canadian Wildlife Service, Environment Canada (3.75 km).
- Ward Falls Trail, owned by C. Ernest Harrison and Sons Ltd. (6 km).
- The Mi'kmaq Wisqoq Trail, Acadian Trail, United Empire Loyalists Trail, and Huguenot Trail run about 4 kilometres altogether and connect with the Trans-Canada Trail. There are interpretive panels along the trail, inscribed in both English and Mi'kmaq.

Did you know...

...that Squally Point, located in the Chignecto day-use park, is an actual raised beach that was created when glaciers covered much of the area?

Largest in Cumberland County
Largest in Nova Scotia

Cape Chignecto, at 4,200 hectares (or 10,000 acres), is Nova Scotia's largest provincial park. A 48-kilometre hiking trail circumnavigates the cape along cliffs that rise up to 200 metres above the Bay of Fundy.

The Three Sisters rock formations at Cape Chignecto

The Streets Where We Live

Amherst streets that have changed their names:

Once called	Now called
Back Street	Church Street
Chandler Street	Prince Arthur Street
Eddy Road	Eddy Street
Halifax Road	Willow Street
Main's Lane	Regent Street
Main Street	Victoria Street
Park Road	East Pleasant Street
Railway Station Road	Crescent Avenue
Tupper Street	Robie Street
The road to the fort	Lawrence Street

Where Did that Name Come From?

In Amherst

- **Rupert Street** was named for Rupert Bent, the member of a prominent local family.
- **Clarence Street** was named for Clarence Silliker, a director of the Silliker Car Company in Halifax, who was originally from Amherst.
- **Dickey Street** was named for Senator R. B. Dickey, a Father of Confederation, who was born in Amherst.
- **Adelaide Street** was named for Adelaide of Saxe-Meiningen, Consort of King William IV (1830–1837).
- **Wellington Street** was named for the Duke of Wellington.

Did you know...

...that the street signs in Pugwash are printed in both Gaelic and English?

In Joggins

* **Dump Road:** guess where this leads to?
* **Hardscrabble Road:** many communities in North America have named a road or area Hardscrabble, usually in reference to poor farmland or the difficulty in making a living there.

In River Hebert

* **Pearl Street** was named for Pearl Keith, a young woman whose family lived there.

In Parrsboro

* **Whitehall Road** was named for Whitehall Road in Westminster, London, England. Its name was, in turn, derived from the Palace of Whitehall, destroyed in 1698.

People

Just the Facts Ma'am

The median age of Cumberland County residents is 45.4.
(StatsCan 2006 Census)

Who We Are, How We Got Here

Mi'kmaq

The Mi'kmaq are members of the Algonquian linguistic indigenous tribe of eastern Canada. Their ancestors, the Paleo-Indians, lived in what is now Cumberland County approximately 10,000 years ago.

For thousands of years the Mi'kmaq lived very much as their ancestors did, as nomadic hunters and gatherers, dependent upon the changing seasons and the natural bounty they supplied. In the winter the Mi'kmaq moved inland to hunt and to shelter from the weather. They built wigwams, constructed of a dome-shaped arrangement of poles covered with birch bark with a fire pit situated in the center. The Mi'kmaq usually spent the other seasons close to the open sea, catching fish with nets or weirs, or lancing them by torchlight. In the summer their homes were rectangular in shape and covered with woven reeds.

The Mi'kmaq called themselves *Lnu'k*, meaning the people.

Mi'kmaq comes from a word in their own language that means "my friends." They visualized their language using pictographs.

According to Nova Scotia ethnologist and linguist Silas Rand (1810–1889), the Mi'kmaq called their county *Megumage*. It included much of present-day Nova Scotia and New Brunswick. The Mi'kmaq were part of the historic Wabanaki Confederacy, which included present-day New England and the Maritime provinces. In order to communicate with each other over this vast area, they developed a system of runners—young men who would go from village to village with news of events, gatherings, and calls to war. For travels by water they made and used wide-bottomed birchbark canoes to cross the Bay of Fundy and the Northumberland Strait.

Did you know...

...that long ago the Mi'kmaq used lobster claws as tobacco pipes?

Acadians

The first French settlers came to Cumberland County in the mid-1600s from western France via Port Royal. These settlers were called Acadians, after the original name for what is now the Maritime provinces. The origin of the word Acadia is obscure, but it may have derived from the Mi'kmaq word *algatig*, meaning fertile land.

The French wished to strengthen their hold on the strategically positioned Isthmus of Chignecto, so settlers were sent into the area to farm. The Acadians quickly set to work reclaiming land from the sea by constructing a system of dykes, or aboiteaux, as they had done in France and along the Minas Basin. As time passed, the Acadians spread out from their initial location in Beaubassin to Minudie, River Hebert, and Joggins. Many became friends with the Mi'kmaq.

The British did not trust the Acadians to remain neutral during their struggle with the French for dominance in North America. Their solution to the problem was evacuation, and in the summer of 1755, they undertook the systematic removal of the Acadians from British territory. About 1,000 Acadians in Minudie, River Hebert, Joggins, Nappan, Maccan, and outlying areas were rounded up and transported by ship. Many families were separated in preparation for the voyage and never saw each other again. Some escaped to the woods and tried to rebuild their lives after the British armies left. Most of those who remained ended up working the land for others as tenant farmers.

Planters

Planters, an old English word for colonists or settlers, were New Englanders who moved north into Nova Scotia, including Cumberland County, between 1759 and 1768, answering the British call to settle in the lands once occupied by the Acadians. For the most part they came from Connecticut, Rhode Island, and Massachusetts, attracted by the rich dykelands of Chignecto and the farmland lying along rivers. Many of the Planters settled in the Maccan and River Hebert area and along the River Philip.

Yorkshiremen

Many settlers from the northern English county of Yorkshire migrated to Cumberland County between 1771 and 1775. Like the Planters, they too were attracted by the fertile marshlands of the Isthmus of Chignecto. Many Yorkshiremen were staunch Methodists who settled in the Nappan area.

Loyalists

The Loyalists—Americans loyal to the British Crown—fled north after much mistreatment at the hands of American patriots during and after the American Revolution. The majority were tradesmen, craftsmen, or farmers. Many purchased farms on the Isthmus of Chignecto, while others settled in Maccan, Nappan, and River Philip.

African-Canadians

The first people of African descent to arrive in what is now Cumberland County came in the early 1700s as slaves of white settlers, usually as domestic workers and farmhands.

The earliest recorded reference to slavery in Amherst was in 1771. In 1776, there was a Black female slave working in Samuel Wethered's Tavern, located within walking distance of Fort Beauséjour. By 1800, slavery had ceased to be protected by law in Nova Scotia. It was then that the provincial court denied slaveholders the right to regain possession of any runaway slaves. In 1833 slavery was officially abolished in the British Empire.

The largest influx of Black immigrants occurred between 1782 and 1785, when about 3,500 arrived in Nova Scotia and New Brunswick as Loyalists. Many had fought for the British in return for their freedom from slavery and they came north to start a new life.

Scots

The first Scots to come to Cumberland County likely migrated from the Pictou area of Nova Scotia or Cape Breton, where they first arrived in the mid-to-late 1770s. Many left Scotland due to the weakening of the traditional clan system and most became farmers in their new home.

Irish

In the early 1760s a number of settlers from Ulster, in the north of Ireland, settled in Cumberland County. Most of the Irish immigrants to Cumberland County arrived during and after the Potato Famine of the 1840s. They arrived by ship in Saint John and Halifax and many, like the Scots, were farmers.

Born Here... Did That

Wayne "Rocky Johnson" Bowles: Born in Amherst, August 24, 1944

Professional wrestler. Wrestled for the National Wrestling Alliance and the World Wrestling Federation, where he was a top contender during the 1970s and 1980s. A popular and effective tag team wrestler, Johnson was inducted into the World Wrestling Entertainment Hall of Fame on March 29, 2008. He is the father of retired professional wrestler and actor, Dwayne "The Rock" Johnson.

Willard S. Boyle: Born in Amherst, August 19, 1924

Physicist and inventor. In 1962 Boyle invented the first continuously operating ruby laser with Don Nelson, and was named on the first patent for a semiconductor injection laser. He was made director of Space Science and Exploratory Studies at the Bell Labs subsidiary, Bellcomm, providing support for the Apollo space program and helping to select lunar landing sites.

William Knapp Buckley: Born in Wallace, date unknown; died 1978

Pharmacist and creator of Buckley's Mixture. W. K. moved to Toronto in 1914 to attend the Ontario College of Pharmacists. In 1919 he developed his famous "it tastes awful but it works" mixture. The following year he formed W. K. Buckley Limited and began to sell his cough and cold remedy.

Fred S. Cameron: Born in Advocate Harbour, 1887; died in British Columbia in 1952

Long-distance runner and winner of the 1910 Boston Marathon. For his effort he was presented with the keys to the City of Boston. He defeated 185 participants from around the world and was described in the *Boston Globe* as the "darkest of dark horses."

Fred Cameron of Advocate winning the Boston Marathon, April 19, 1910

Charles Aubrey Eaton: Born in Pugwash, 1868; died in Washington, D.C., January 23, 1953

Preacher and politician. In 1904, he was arrested on the streets of Cleveland, Ohio, for ignoring bylaws prohibiting street preaching. As a result of his religious work in Cleveland, he came to the attention of John D. Rockefeller. They became lifelong friends. In 1924, Eaton was elected as a Republican, serving until 1952. He signed the original United Nations Charter as part of a delegation representing the U.S. government.

Cyrus Eaton: Born in Pugwash, December 27, 1883; died in Ohio, May 9, 1979

Investment banker, businessman, and philanthropist. A protegé of John D. Rockefeller and acquaintance of philosopher Bertrand Russell, Eaton offered his hometown of Pugwash as the location of a conference to discuss the dangers of nuclear weapons, which had been called for in the 1955 Russell-Einstein Manifesto. The first meeting, thereafter known as the Pugwash Conference on Science and World Affairs, was held in July 1957. It meets each year at Thinker's Lodge in Pugwash, Eaton's former summer home.

Thinker's Lodge in Pugwash, former home of Cyrus Eaton

Leslie Feist: Born in Amherst, February 13, 1976

Internationally known singer and songwriter. Her father, artist Harold Feist, was teaching at Mount Allison University in Sackville, New Brunswick, in 1976, and her mother Lyn travelled to the maternity ward of the Highland View Hospital in Amherst to give birth. In 2007 Feist was nominated for four Grammy Awards, including best new artist. In 2008 she won five Juno Awards, including artist of the year.

Donald (Sandy) Goss: Born in Amherst, October 2, 1968

International freestyle and backstroke swimmer. He competed in the Olympic Summer Games in Los Angeles in 1984, and in Seoul in 1988. On both occasions he won the silver medal with the men's 4 x 100 medley relay team.

Ross Hamilton: Born in Pugwash, 1889; died in Halifax, September 29, 1965

National celebrity and member of the original cast of the Dumbells. The Dumbells was a Canadian vaudeville troupe formed in 1917 near Vimy Ridge by 10 members of the Canadian Army's Third Division to raise morale for the troops. Its name was derived from the division's emblem, a red dumbbell. The group sang, danced, and staged plays, often as female impersonators—Ross's stage name was Marjorie. After the front lines of France and Belgium, they performed for King Albert of Belgium and at the Coliseum in London. Returning to North America in 1919, they appeared at the Ambassador Theater in New York and completed 12 cross-Canada tours. The troupe disbanded in 1932.

(Percy) Wyndham Lewis: Born near Amherst, November 18, 1882; died in Britain March 7, 1957

Major twentieth-century British artist and writer. His father, Charles Edward Lewis, was an American lawyer and writer who loved to sail and often visited the Maritime provinces. Lewis contended that he was born on his father's yacht, the *Wanda*, "docked at Amherst, Nova Scotia." Painter Walter Sickert described Lewis as the "greatest portraitist of this or any other time." He painted such luminaries as Edith Sitwell, T. S. Eliot, and Ezra Pound. Indeed, along with Eliot and Pound, Lewis was considered one of the "Big 5" modernist writers, a group that also included W. B. Yeats and James Joyce. He was involved with the Camden Group of painters and clashed with the literary giants of the Bloomsbury Group. During World War I Lewis was a lieutenant in the Royal Artillery and an official war artist.

Helen McCully: Born in Amherst, date unknown; died in New York, 1976

Best remembered in Cumberland County as the author of *The Christmas Pony*, a book about a Victorian-era Christmas in Amherst. However, she was better known in the American culinary world as gourmet, hostess par excellence, recipe creator, author, and mentor to cooking icons Julia Child and James Pepin. Long before Martha Stewart, Helen McCully ruled as one of North America's foremost authorities on elegant living. She was a long-time food editor for both *House Beautiful* and *McCall's Magazine*, and wrote numerous articles and cookbooks, including *Just Desserts* (1961), *American Heritage Cookbook* (1964), and *Waste Not, Want Not* (1975).

PEOPLE

Anne Murray: Born in Springhill, June 20, 1945

Internationally renowned singer, songwriter, and Canadian icon. She is the first Canadian female solo singer to reach number one on the U.S. charts and also the first to earn a gold record (for "Snowbird," one of her signature songs). She is the recipient of four Grammy Awards, three Country Music Association Awards, and countless Junos and American Music Awards.

Anne Murray in the exhibit area of the Anne Murray Centre, Springhill

Peter Myles: Born in Amherst, October 25, 1968

Film music editor. He holds editing credits for numerous film soundtracks, including: *Harry Potter and the Philosopher's Stone*; *Harry Potter and the Chamber of Secrets*; *Harry Potter and the Prisoner of Azkaban*; *Star Wars Episode II: Attack of the Clones*; and *The Bourne Supremacy.*

Simon Newcombe: Born in Wallace, March 12, 1835; died in Washington D.C., July 11, 1909

Astronomer and mathematician. He made important contributions to the fields of astronomy, timekeeping, economics, and statistics. The first person to measure the distance between the planets, he was a charter member and first president of the American Astronomical Society. For 20 years he was the Superintendent of the Ephemeris and Nautical Almanac Office at the U.S. Naval Observatory in Washington. He was buried with military honours in Arlington National Cemetery with President William H. Taft in attendance.

William Arthur O'Donnell: Born in Springhill, May 4, 1948

Harness racer. O'Donnell was given the nickname Magic for being able to drive a horse seemingly past its limitations. He was named Harness Tracks of America's Driver of the Year in 1984 and set a yearly earnings record of over $9 million. The next year, he became harness racing's first driver to eclipse $10 million in earnings in a single year.

James Layton Ralston: Born in Amherst, September 27, 1881; died in Montreal, May 21, 1948

Lawyer, soldier, and politician. Ralston served in World War I as an officer in the North Nova Scotia Highlanders and was decorated for bravery. In 1924 he was appointed to the cabinet by Prime Minister William Lyon Mackenzie King and became minister of national defence. The Colonel James L. Ralston Armoury in Amherst is named in his honour.

Famous Residents

J. F. W. DesBarres (1721–1824) was one of the largest landowners in what became the Maritime provinces. In 1765 he received a grant for 7,000 acres of land at Minudie, and for 8,000 in Nappan and the Maccan Valley. He lived in Nappan between 1812 and 1817. He was a surveyor for the British and was also the lieutenant-governor of Cape Breton and Prince Edward Island. Legend has it that in celebration of his 100th birthday, DesBarres danced a jig on a tavern table.

Wilf Carter (1904–1996) was a country music singer, songwriter, and yodeller. He lived in River Hebert between 1912 and 1916 when his father, Reverend Henry Carter, was the Baptist minister there. Carter made his radio debut in Calgary in 1930. He went on to have a successful career in both Canada and the U.S., where he was known as Montana Slim. He has been called the father of country music in Canada.

Alex Colville (1920–) is an internationally renowned realist painter. The Colville family moved from Toronto to Amherst when Alex was nine years old and he lived there until 1938, when he enrolled at Mount Allison University in Sackville, New Brunswick. From 1944 to 1946 he was a war artist with the Canadian Forces overseas. After the war he taught art at Mount Allison University from 1946 until 1963, when he retired to pursue painting full-time. Colville holds eight honorary degrees and the Order of Canada.

Abraham Gesner (1797–1864) was a physician, surgeon, geologist, and inventor. During the 1830s he practised medicine in Parrsboro. He chose to live in the area due to its interesting geology. Gesner is best known as the developer and patent holder of a process for manufacturing kerosene, which took the place of whale oil for the lighting of lamps. For this reason he is often credited with saving the sperm whale from extinction.

Amos "King" Seaman, date unknown

Amos "King" Seaman (1788–1864) was a landowner, entrepreneur, philanthropist, and poet. At the age of eight he ran away from home by sailing across the Cumberland Basin from Sackville, NB, to Cumberland County. As a youth he worked on the wharfs of Boston and in 1810 he started the A. Seaman Company, which shipped hay and vegetables from Minudie to Boston and the Caribbean. He later expanded his interests to grindstones, land ownership, and mercantile. During his later years he was one of the wealthiest men in the county. A lover of the finer things in life, he built a mansion for his family at Minudie and had a second home in Boston's fashionable Beacon Hill. He cultivated friendships with Sir Charles Tupper, Joseph Howe, and Henry Wadsworth Longfellow. Seaman fancied himself as something of a poet and would often write orders for his employees in rhyming verse.

Brook Watson (1735–1807) came from Boston to Fort Lawrence in the early 1750s. He lived in the area for four years as a trader's helper, secretary, and accountant. Author Will R. Bird tells the story that, in 1755, some cattle swam over to the French side of the Missiquash River. Watson got them back to Fort Lawrence by swimming across the river and herding them before the French army was aware of his presence. This feat, which saved the English their winter's supply of meat, was all the more notable due to the fact that Watson was missing the lower half of his right leg. In 1749, at the age of 14, he had been attacked by a shark in Havana Harbour and the limb had to be amputated. Watson quickly moved up the military and political ranks and in 1796 he was made Lord Mayor of London. He commissioned his friend, renowned portrait painter John Singleton Copley, to commemorate the Havana incident and the result was Copley's famous 1778 painting *Watson and the Shark*.

Did you know...

...that playwright and actor Sam Shepherd once owned a home in Advocate?

...that actress Megan Follows still does?

They Slept Here: Famous Visitors

1398

It is said that **Prince Henry Sinclair, the Earl of Orkney** (c.1345–1400), visited the area now known as Advocate Harbour, supposedly in search of the Holy Grail. Sinclair is presumed to have built a new ship while in the area and returned to the Orkneys with it.

About 1607

Samuel de Champlain (c.1574–1635) also visited Advocate Harbour, which he called Port of Mines, in search of copper. He took amethyst off the beaches in the area to present to King Henry IV of France.

1882

Oscar Wilde (1854–1900) visited Amherst as part of a North American tour. Wilde was on the lecture circuit expounding the aesthetic movement and the theory of "art for art's sake." According to a newspaper account, he called Amherst "a pretty little town."

He had no interest in the ruins of Fort Cumberland, though, as the battles fought there "were not fought for love of beauty, but for the love of territory." Amherst was interested in "Wilde Oscar," as he was called then, and people flocked to the train station to meet him. However the general consensus of the people of Amherst, as reprinted in the *Citizen* in 1973, was that Oscar's hair "was not good. It was the colour of straw...faded and bleached looking and when not looked after goes climbing all over his features."

1917

Leon Trotsky (1879–1940) was Vladimir Lenin's right-hand man and a military strategist instrumental in spearheading the 1917 October Revolution in Russia. Months before, he had been the unwilling guest of the Amherst Internment Camp. On April 1, 1917, the ship *Christianiafjord*, en route from New York to Europe and carrying Trotsky and his family, arrived in Halifax. The naval police detained Trotsky as a security risk, and after some questioning transported him (his family remained in Halifax) to Amherst, where he was incarcerated in the Malleable Iron Foundry building on the corner of Park and Hickman Streets. Trotsky was in Amherst for a month with approximately 800 other inmates, most of whom were German sailors who had been captured in the Atlantic. While the British and Russian governments tried to sort out Trotsky's removal from the camp, he spent his time teaching his fellow prisoners about Marxism, translating the *Halifax Chronicle* into Russian and German, and giving speeches. He was popular with the prisoners. On April 29 he was released and allowed to continue his journey. Trotsky would later say of the experience, "Even now it makes me happy to remember that in the very midst of war, we were fraternizing with German soldiers in Amherst."

1939

George VI (1895–1952) and **Queen Elizabeth** (1900–2002) visited Cumberland County during the month-long Royal Tour of May and June 1939. It was the first time that a reigning monarch had visited

Canada. The tour was conducted almost entirely by train, and stops in the county included Springhill and Amherst.

About 1943

During the exile of the Dutch monarchy to Britain in World War II, **Princess Juliana of the Netherlands** (1909–2004) stayed for a brief period at Ottawa House "By-the-Sea" in Parrsboro. She and her two eldest children lived for a year in Ottawa and she was invited to tour Nova Scotia by the provincial government.

1958

Prince Philip (1921–), **Duke of Edinburgh**, visited Springhill on October 30, 1958, in the wake of the "bump" in Springhill Mine No. 2. He was attending meetings in Ottawa and came to the devastated town to lend moral support.

1961

Soviet cosmonaut **Yuri Gagarin** (1934–1968) made a trip to Pugwash after his famous April 1961 space flight. He chose Pugwash, home of the Pugwash Conference on Science and World Affairs, as his only stop in Canada.

1980

Terry Fox (1958–1981) stayed overnight in Wentworth during his 1980 cross-country Marathon of Hope.

2006

Bill Clinton (1946–), president of the United States from 1993 to 2001, was a guest speaker at a symposium held at the Fox Harb'r Spa and Resort.

Not Always "Avon Calling"

Itinerant peddlers were commonplace in Cumberland County throughout most of its history until automobile ownership allowed many rural communities easy access to shops in larger centres. Today there are still a few individuals in the county who sell meat, fish, and vegetables door-to-door.

Perhaps the best-known Cumberland County peddler was **Moses Barrett** (about 1805–1864), who was likely born in New England and moved first to Yarmouth and later to Amherst. Barrett's business was clocks, and he sold them in Cumberland County and New Brunswick between around 1820 and 1840. Barrett did not make any of the clocks he sold, but was a sales agent for a number of New England clockmakers. He would often buy movements and cases separately and put them together in his workshop. Researchers Jane Varkaris and James Connell say that "in a survey of clocks in Canada conducted in 1978, there were more clocks reported in private collections and museums with the name Moses Barrett on the labels than any other individual's name." Moses Barrett may have endeared himself to customers with his love of small talk, his cat that accompanied him on his travels, and his preference for eating whole pumpkin pies in one sitting. He has been identified as the possible inspiration for Thomas Haliburton's 1836 book, *The Clockmaker, or the Sayings and Doings of Samuel Slick.* Haliburton himself admitted that he "first met Sam Slick...somewhere between Colchester County and Fort Lawrence, near Amherst."

Mary Mansour (d.1925) was a popular peddler in Shulie in the early part of the twentieth century. Originally from Lebanon, Mary would sell needles and thread and a variety of other small items. She was nicknamed "Two Monday" as she would inform her customers that she would return in "two Monday," meaning in two weeks' time.

Moses Sorge (d.1950) was a clothes peddler in the 1930s and 1940s. He travelled out from Amherst to other parts of the county, walking from house to house and carrying a pack on his back. He sold a variety of clothing and housewares, including dresses, underwear, socks, shirts, bobby pins, hairnets, and towels.

Watson Weaver (1895–1972) was a peddler from the 1920s well into the 1940s. From his home in Springhill he would travel the county on foot, selling household items such as mittens, pot holders, and pillowcases handmade by his sister Erma. His bestselling items, however, were the photographs he took with his trusty Kodak camera. Watson would shoot county landscapes, events, ships, natural disasters, and people. He worked hard to get photographs of any celebrity visiting the province, including Queen Elizabeth II and World War II Field Marshal Bernard Montgomery. Today many Cumberland County homes likely have a Watson Weaver photograph in their collections. Like Moses Barrett, Weaver seems to have had the "gift of gab" and would regale his customers with news and gossip from the communities he travelled through.

They Cared For US

Doctors and Nurses

Minnie A. Follette (d.1918), of Port Greville, was a nurse during World War I. She died when the hospital ship *Letitia* was torpedoed off the Irish coast. It was returning to Europe from Halifax, where it had delivered wounded soldiers back home.

Dr. Ram Boodoosingh was a popular family doctor in River Hebert for over 25 years. Each year at graduation the Dalhousie University medical school offers the Dr. Ram Singari Boodoosingh Memorial Prize, an annual book prize awarded to a graduating medical student who, "with clinical skill and a sense of humour, most brings

First in Cumberland County First in Canada

Charles Tupper was the founder and first president of the Canadian Medical Association.

Sir Charles Tupper, 1893

art to the practice of medicine." Each June, the River Hebert District High School awards the Dr. Ram Boodoosingh Memorial Prize.

Miss Elizabeth Jane and **Miss Frances Newman** were the first graduates of the All Saints Hospital Nursing Training School in Springhill. The school opened in 1893 and operated until 1947.

Midwives

Abigail Reid Roblee, a midwife from Streets Ridge

Abigail Reid Roblee (1829–1912) lived for approximately 60 years in Streets Ridge. She ministered to the sick of the area, tended children with diphtheria, and prepared the dead for burial. She was also a popular midwife and delivered many babies in her lifetime.

Lalia Leger (1917–2008), born in Chignecto, was a midwife who delivered over 100 babies in the River Hebert area.

Our Own Florence Nightingale

Adeliza A. Betts, from Wallace, became known as the "Lady with the Lamp." During World War I she was superintendent of the Deaconess Hospital in Boston.

In Deed!

What a Drag!

On October 15, 1927, Frank Elliot and George Scott, of Amherst, finished their trek across Canada in their Model T Ford. The car was towed 4,759 miles across the country in 89 days.

Did you know...

...that Eldon George registered his Parrsboro Rock and Mineral Shop in 1948, making it the oldest establishment of its kind in Canada?

...that on April 10, 1984, at Wasson's Bluff, he unearthed trackways of the world's smallest dinosaur?

Don't Mess with These Guys

Haiman Simpson of Springhill held the heavyweight boxing title in the Canadian Expeditionary Force during World War I, while John Letcher of Springhill was the lightweight champion.

Nobel Deeds

British nuclear physicist Dr. Joseph Rotblat and the Pugwash Conference on Science and World Affairs were awarded the Nobel Peace Prize in 1995.

Order Please

Cumberland County natives and residents who have...

...been awarded the Order of Canada:

Diligent River

* Harry Ward, World War II veteran. Founded the Quebec division of the Canadian Paraplegic Association.

Malagash

* Lorne O. Clarke, Canadian lawyer and former chief justice of the Nova Scotia Supreme Court

Oxford

* John Bragg, entrepreneur

Pugwash

* Norman Archibald Macrae Mackenzie (1894–1986), lawyer and professor
* Dennice Leahey, corporate leader
* Irwin William (I. W.) Akerley (1904–1995), businessman and politician

Springhill

* Anne Murray, singer, songwriter

...been awarded the Order of Nova Scotia:

Malagash

* Lorne O. Clarke. In 1998–99, he was the chair of the Memorial Advisory Committee of Swissair Flight 111.

Springhill

* Dr. Robert Arnold Burden. First physician to go underground during the 1956 Springhill mining disaster.
* Anne Murray. The first woman and the first Canadian to win Album of the Year at the Country Music Association Awards for her 1984 album, *A Little Good News*.

PEOPLE

...won other prestigious awards:

* Maurice Ruddick, the "Singing Miner" of Springhill (1913–1988) was named Canada's Citizen of the Year in recognition of his bravery during the Springhill "bump" of 1958.
* Johnny Mooring of Springhill won the Canadian Open Old Time Fiddle Championship three years in a row: 1964, 1965, and 1966.
* In 1972, Henry Lindsay Christie from Wallace Bay was the first person to win the American Scientific Glassblowers Society J. Alexander Award for his outstanding contribution to furthering the aims and ideals of the ASGS.

Fearless Leaders?

Prime Time

Sir Charles Tupper was Canada's sixth prime minister. He holds the record for the shortest time in office: 69 days.

Did you know...

...that Cumberland County was the birthplace of four Fathers of Confederation?
From Amherst: **E. B. Chandler** (1800–1880)
R. B. Dickey (1811–1903)
Charles Tupper (1821–1915)
From near Nappan: **Jonathan McCully** (1809–1877)

Premier Event

- Sir Charles Tupper, premier of the colony of Nova Scotia, 1864–1867; premier of the province of Nova Scotia, 1867.
- William Thomas Pipes (1850–1909)—born in Amherst—premier of Nova Scotia, 1882–1884.
- Edgar Nelson Rhodes (1877–1942)—born in Amherst—premier of Nova Scotia, 1925–1930.
- Roger Bacon (1926–)—born in Upper Nappan—premier of Nova Scotia, 1990–1991.

At Your Service

Robert Coates served as the MP for Cumberland County for 31 years, winning 11 elections. He is the fifth-longest serving MP.

Good Knight

Charles Tupper received a knighthood in 1867.

Eureka!

Willard Boyle, from Wallace, holds 16 patents, one of which was used for the Hubble Space Telescope.

George W. Leadbetter of Springhill invented the replaceable pool cue tip. Patent number CA 198,960, April 6, 1920.

First in Cumberland County First in Canada

Henry Danson of Springhill was the first Canadian soldier to be decorated in World War I. He was awarded the Distinguished Conduct Medal.

Major Anthony (Tony) Condy of Springhill was the first Canadian soldier to be decorated in World War II. He received the British Empire Medal from King George VI during a ceremony at Buckingham Palace.

In 1899 **Professor Max Sterne** of Lower Cove, along with Amherst entrepreneur **Clarence Silliker**, marketed (and may have created) a device for applying a wood grain finish to inexpensive woods.

PEOPLE

Cumberland County Firsts

The Curry Family

Senator Nathanial Curry's Lorneville mansion contained Cumberland County's first saltwater swimming pool. His brother, Albert S. Curry, was the first owner of an automobile in Amherst, and the vice-president of the Rhodes, Curry Company that produced it.

Where's the Remote?

Allison Smith of Parrsboro is thought to have owned the first TV in Cumberland County.

Women First

Margaret Jewett of River Hebert was the first female county councillor of Cumberland County.

Ruth Allen of Advocate was the first female warden of Cumberland County.

Did you know...

...that Mount Kerr, in Jasper Park, Alberta, is named for Fox River native John "Chip" Kerr (1887–1964), who received the Victoria Cross—the highest award for valour in the British Commonwealth—on February 5, 1917? He captured 62 prisoners and 250 yards of enemy trench. Kerr was the first Nova Scotian to be so honoured.

They Had a Hand In It

Name Game

Jollymore Corner in Cape Chignecto Park was named by Bill Jollymore of River Hebert.

Did you know...

...that McDonald's McLobster Roll was developed by Gerry Moore of Amherst?

...that Blake Riley from Amherst performed in the Broadway production of *Miss Saigon* between 1997 and 2000?

Teachers

Caroline (Yates) Ratchford (1813–1889) established the Amherst Female Seminary in 1852. She and her sister were described in the newspapers of the time as "ladies in every sense of the word and highly educated."

First in Cumberland County First in Canada

Philopina (Atkinson) Betts (d.1863) of Wallace was the first woman to teach public school in Nova Scotia.

This Just In

The top three Cumberland County newsmakers of the last 20 years according to Darrell Cole, senior editor of the *Amherst Daily News*:

1. Bill Casey, former Cumberland–Colchester–Musquodoboit Valley MP
2. Jerry Hallee, former Amherst mayor
3. Ernie Fage, former Cumberland North MLA

Society and Culture

Food for Thought

* The Mi'kmaq, Cumberland County's first inhabitants, dug clams, mussels, and oysters and hunted shad, bass, salmon, and gaspereau. They ate wild roots and plants, carrots and potatoes. For a treat they boiled down sap in earthen pots to make maple sugar cakes.
* Rappie pie, *pâté à la râpure*, is a popular Acadian dish made of meat, such as moose or venison, potatoes, onions, seasoning, and other ingredients according to taste.
* Dinner was, and in some families still is, traditionally the noon meal in Cumberland County. It used to be the main meal of the day and kept farmers going until suppertime.
* Supper, in many homes, is the last full meal of the day, usually eaten between 4:00 PM and 6:00 PM.
* Lunch often refers to a snack in the evening, usually just before bed, sometimes called a "bed lunch." It traditionally consisted of tea and sandwiches or sweets; sometimes it was a moose or deer steak. Today it's more likely to be pop and chips. A lunch is always eaten during a card party or evening gathering.
* A certain housekeeper in Oxford would create cinnamon pops by pouring hot water over cinnamon on toast.

We're Cookin' Now

Sarah Glenn (1908–2004) of Lower Cove baked doughnuts by the hundreds. She sold many of them to loyal customers from Cumberland County, the Annapolis Valley, Ontario, and Alberta. At the age of 89 she baked 109 dozen for Christmas orders, and kept making doughnuts until the age of 92. The ingredients she used were common to all doughnut recipes; her secret was in the beating of the batter—she did it a lot. Her daughter-in-law Annie Glenn supplied this method from her observation of the process, but try as we might, none of us will be able to make them as Sarah did.

Sarah Glenn's Doughnuts

2 eggs, well beaten
1 cup sugar
5 tablespoons melted margarine
3 cups flour
3 teaspoons baking powder
½ teaspoon salt
1 cup milk
1 teaspoon vanilla

Be sure all ingredients are at room temperature. Beat eggs well. Add sugar a little at a time. Add melted margarine, continue beating well. Sift flour, baking powder, and salt together; add a little at a time with a little milk. Add vanilla last. Roll out on board. Cut with doughnut cutter. Do not twist cutter. Fry in hot lard to a golden brown. Sprinkle with sugar, if desired.

Ernest Thompson of Street's Ridge would pour molasses over fried eggs, a habit he picked up from working in Cumberland County lumber camps.

This following use of molasses might be more to your liking:

Sarah Burbine's Gingerbread

½ cup white sugar
1 egg
½ cup shortening or butter
1 cup molasses
1 ½ teaspoon baking soda
1 teaspoon cloves
½ teaspoon salt
1 teaspoon cinnamon
1 teaspoon ginger
1 ½ cups flour
1 cup hot water
raisins (as many as desired)

Cream shortening and sugar, add beaten eggs, and molasses. Add dry ingredients with hot water. Add raisins. Put in greased long pan. Bake at 350°F (180°C) for 45 minutes or until done.

Try this from Cumberland County's only winery:

Mussels Steamed in Muscat Butter

1 carrot, diced
1 onion, diced
1 red pepper, diced
4 garlic cloves, minced
1 lemon, sliced
2 cups Eagle Tree Muscat (just ensure there is adequate liquid in the pan for steaming)
1 cup cream
fresh chives and parsley

In a large fry pan, sauté the first 5 ingredients. Add the wine and mussels, increase heat, and cover. Cook until the mussels open. Finish with a dash of cream and a sprinkle of chopped chives and parsley.

From www.jostwine.com

Cumberland County Cake

1 ¼ cups maple syrup
2 eggs
½ teaspoon vanilla
1 cup flour
⅛ teaspoon ground coriander
1 teaspoon baking powder
dash of salt

Gently boil the maple syrup for one minute and set aside. Separate eggs. Beat the egg whites well and then the egg yolks. Add vanilla to the yolks. Add yolks to the maple syrup. Fold in egg whites. Sift together dry ingredients and fold into above mixture. Place batter in Bundt pan. Bake about 1 hour at 325°F (160°C). Cool at least 1 hour on a rack, and then remove from pan. Top with sprinkled confectioner's sugar or your favourite icing.

From www.mmmaple.com

Bake with blueberries, Cumberland County's most famous food:

Blueberry Crisp

3 cups blueberries
2 tablespoons lemon juice
⅔ cup brown sugar
½ cup flour
½ cup oatmeal
⅓ cup butter, softened
¾ teaspoon cinnamon

Preheat oven to 375°F (190°C). Put blueberries in ungreased 8 x 8 inch pan. Sprinkle with lemon juice. Mix brown sugar, flour, oatmeal, butter, and cinnamon. Sprinkle over berries. Bake for 30 minutes. Serve warm or cold with ice cream, or cooled with whipped cream.

Maureen Glennie, *What's Cooking in Advocate & Area?*

Drink without Thought

Historian Ernest Clark describes the heavy alcohol intake at eighteenth-century Fort Beauséjour:

- In summer [drinking was] a diversion from mosquitoes; in winter [it was] shelter from the cold.
- The American Revolution disrupted the importing of rum into the Maritimes and the War of 1812 turned the rum trade into a large smuggling industry.
- In 1840, 82 women from Cumberland County signed a petition stating that they "would consider their happiness in this world consummate if the Monster alcohol was banished [from] our land."
- On October 27, 1881, the *Chignecto Post* reported: "A large group here drink on only two occasions: when they have goose for dinner, and when they don't."

Arts and Entertainment

What a Performance!

Fraser's Hall Shows was Springhill's first theatre. The Maple Players Theatre Group of Oxford formed in 1975; they perform two productions a year.

The Little Ferry That Could

On Wednesday evenings in 1934, Cooper's Orchestra entertained passengers during moonlight cruises on the *Kipawo*, a 113-foot passenger and freight ferry that sailed the Minas Basin during the 1920s and 1930s. Its name was derived from the three ports it served: Kingsport, Parrsboro, and Wolfville.

In 1941 the *Kipawo* was drafted into the Royal Canadian Navy and served in the Montreal Naval Yard. It also worked as a naval inspection

The *Kipawo*, home of Ship's Company Theatre, Parrsboro

ship and later guarded St. John's Harbour and the waters off Bell Island, Newfoundland. Up until 1977, when it was run aground, the *Kip* ferried passengers from Bell Island to Portugal Cove. In 1982 it was discovered by a Parrsboro native and salvaged back to its old home in Cumberland County.

In 1984, Michael Fuller and Mary Vingoe, co-founders of the Ship's Company Theatre, staged their first production upon the *Kipawo*.

All Kinds of Fun

The Mi'kmaq used to meet in Malagash once a year for games and contests in archery, wrestling, and foot racing. They would dance and play waltes, a traditional dice game.

There were other forms of entertainment in the county. According to the August 14, 1884, *Chignecto Post*:

> At an old fashioned entertainment held at the Minudie Music Hall, a pair of saddlebags excited much interest. They were the ones in which a Mr. McElmon carried the mail from Truro to Fort Lawrence some 70 years ago. The bags bore the date 1763. He never stopped in Amherst because there were only three houses there. Some of the china and mantel ornaments on display in the hall were over 160 years old.

Read All About It

The Cumberland Regional Library was founded in 1967. It consists of 7 branches located in Advocate, Amherst, Oxford, Parrsboro, Pugwash, River Hebert, and Springhill. Twenty-two per cent of the residents of Cumberland County are registered with the library, and in 2007 approximately 155,000 items were borrowed from the library collection.

Moving Pictures

The Grandview Drive-In, located just outside Amherst, operated from 1955 to 1983.

Did you know...

...that some scenes from the 1986 movie *Children of a Lesser God*, starring William Hurt and Marlee Matlin, were shot at the Interprovincial School for the Education of the Deaf in Amherst?

Writers in Residence

Grace McLeod Rogers (1865–1958) lived for a time in Amherst. She wrote short stories and various historical texts, and was a leading member of the women's movement in the first decades of the twentieth century. She was the mother of the Honourable Norman McLeod Rogers.

Will R. Bird (1891–1984) was born in East Mapleton. He wrote extensively about Cumberland County, often disguising place names in his novels. In *So Much to Record* (1951), he called Parrsboro "Carrsboro" and named one of his female characters Shulie. In *Here Stays Good Yorkshire* (1945), Athol was renamed "Bathol." During his career he wrote over 500 stories.

Bertha Scott (d.2002) and **Jean Heffernan** (c.1900–1981), both from Springhill, wrote books and newspaper articles that played important roles in preserving the history and folklore of the town.

Getting Around

Watch Where You're Going

On April 1, 1923, Nova Scotia switched to driving on the right-hand side of the road from the left. The trouble was that New Brunswick had made the change on December 1, 1922, so for four months drivers had to be sure to switch from one side of the road to the other when they crossed the provincial border.

Communications

The Saint John Stage Coach Company began regular runs between Saint John, New Brunswick, and Amherst in 1836. Travellers would have one overnight stop in Petitcodiac and arrive in Amherst the next evening.

By November 1849, the running of telegraph lines through Amherst to Halifax ended New Brunswick's pony express service.

Before the twentieth century, messages were sent from Isle de Haute to Advocate Harbour by lighting signal fires.

SOCIETY

It's Traditional

Medical Purposes

Ginger and molasses were taken to soothe a sore throat, while a hot lemon drink made the patient sweat out fever or cold.

Christmas Traditions

Years ago, many people in Cumberland County would not trim their tree until Christmas Eve. In some families with small children, Santa would trim the tree and the children would not see it decorated until the morning of the big day. Author Helen McCully notes this in her 1967 children's book, *The Christmas Pony*, about an Amherst Christmas. She recounts "the children never saw the decorated tree until the morning of Christmas."

In Lower Cove, some families had the tradition of hanging up their stockings on New Year's Eve instead of Christmas Eve. It was Mrs. Claus who filled them with candy and small toys.

In Amherst the New Year's Baby was known to leave gifts in your slippers on New Year's Eve.

Also popular in the county was the New Year's Day tradition of having a dark-haired man or boy as the first person to step across the threshold to bring good luck. The visitor would receive a small gift, such as a box of chocolates or pair of socks. In Advocate this practice was called lucky birding. Homeowners would hang gifts outside for the young man to claim. Sometimes the visitor would bring a fir bough with him to hang in the house and this offering would be left hanging over the inside door frame all year for good luck.

Education

Advocate District School is the only Cumberland County school that includes grades primary through to grade 12.

It Happened in...

1937— Good Will No Hunting

The Chignecto Game Sanctuary opened in 1937. It covers 85 square miles.

First in Cumberland County First in Nova Scotia

In 1947 the first rural district high school in Nova Scotia was opened in River Hebert. It was the result of a provincial initiative to improve the standards of rural education.

The Interprovincial School for the Education of the Deaf moved from Halifax to Amherst. Administered jointly by the New Brunswick and Nova Scotia governments, it closed in 1994.

1971—Creation Myth

In 1971 a statue of the Mi'kmaq spirit Glooscap was built in Parrsboro. It is constructed of papier-mâché and fibreglass. Mi'kmaq legend says that Glooscap created many of the land formations in Eastern Canada. He supposedly turned a moose into Isle Haute. Glooscap is also believed to have taught the Mi'kmaq how to make birchbark canoes.

Community Events

- ✻ The Nova Scotia Gem and Mineral Show, formerly known as the Rock-Hound-Roundup, which began in 1965, takes place each August in Parrsboro.
- ✻ The Cumberland County Exhibition, under the auspices of the Oxford Agriculture Society, has been in operation since 1918. The Blueberry Harvest Festival was added to the celebrations in 1988. It is held in late August each year.
- ✻ Both Parrsboro and Springhill hold an Old Home Week in July.
- ✻ The Maritime Stock Breeder's Association held its first winter's fair in Amherst in 1901.
- ✻ The Gathering of Clans and Fisherman's Regatta is held annually in Pugwash on July 1. This Scottish festival began in 1951 as a fundraiser for the Red Cross Hospital.
- ✻ Amherst, Oxford, and Malagash hold events for the Wild Blueberry Harvest Festival, which takes place in July and August each year.
- ✻ The Pugwash Harbourfest takes place at the end of July.

The county's top annual events according to the Cumberland Regional Economic Development Association:

1	Gathering of the Clans	July 1	Pugwash
2	Ship's Company Theatre	Summer	Parrsboro
3	Nova Scotia Gem and Mineral Show	August	Parrsboro
4	Blessing of the Crops	Third Sunday in August	Minudie
5	Cumberland County Exhibition	end of August, beginning September	Oxford

SOCIETY

Our Motto Is:

Cumberland County 4-H clubs: *"Learn to do by doing."*

Sunrise Trail: *"Warm Water, Warm Welcome."*

Amherst and Springhill Rotary Clubs: *"Service above self."*

Town of Amherst: *"Faith in our people, pride in our products."*

Town of Springhill: *"You should see us now."*

Town of Oxford: *"Blueberry Capital of Canada."*

Town of Parrsboro: *"Small Town, Big Heart."*

Village of Pugwash: *"World Famous for Peace."*

Expressions and Impressions

Alicia Anne Jeffrey (d.1864), the daughter of the Honourable Thomas Jeffrey of Halifax, created a series of lithographs of the Parrsboro area in the mid-nineteenth century.

Revolutionary **Leon Trotsky** described the living quarters for prisoners at Amherst Internment Camp in *My Life*, his 1930 autobiography:

> The Amherst concentration camp was located in an old and very dilapidated iron-foundry that had been confiscated from its German owner. The sleeping bunks were arranged in three tiers, two deep, on each side of the hall. About eight hundred of us lived in these conditions. The air in this improvised dormitory at night can be imagined. Men hopelessly clogged the passages, elbowed their way through, lay down or got up, played cards or chess. Many of them practiced crafts, some with extraordinary skill. I still have, stored in Moscow, some things made by Amherst prisoners. And yet, in spite of the heroic efforts of the prisoners to keep themselves physically and morally fit, five of them had gone insane. We had to eat and sleep in the same room as these madmen.

Edith Watson (1860–1944), an American itinerant photographer, fell in love with Canada. In the early years of the twentieth century she travelled across the country with her partner, writer Victoria Hayward, taking photographs and researching their travelogue *Romantic Canada*, published in 1922. During the latter part of World War I they spent time in West Bay, taking photos of the figureheads of the wooden ships that were brought back into service to haul cargo due to the war. Hayward noted, "You can count them three and four deep in West Bay by Partridge Island out of Parrsboro."

Amherst artist **Roberta Taylor** (1905–1990) painted Cumberland County scenes. She was particularly interested in the skies over the Tantramar Marsh and the streetscapes of her hometown. A number of her pieces are in the collection of the Cumberland County Museum.

Helen McCully writes about the Tantramar marsh through the eyes of a young girl in *The Christmas Pony*, stating, "The best way to enjoy the marsh was to be unhappy" and "the marsh was not only marvellous for unhappiness...it was a place for all seasons."

Real Sports

Young and Old Alike

- In 1988, Springhill's Robert Henderson, at age 15, was the youngest person to win the Canadian National Bowling Championship.
- In 1991, Gus Prentice of Springhill won the Canadian Seniors Golf Tournament.
- In 1946, Adam Gray of Joggins won the Nova Scotia Middleweight Boxing Championship.

Did you know...

...that the Shamrocks, a woman's softball team from River Hebert formed in 1933, won the Nova Scotia Women's Softball Championship three years later?

Hockey

- William (Bill) Red Stuart (1900–1978) of Amherst played for the Boston Bruins between 1923 and 1927.
- The 1970–71 Amherst Pee Wee Macs were the first Nova Scotia peewee hockey champions.

Did you know...

...that William (Bill) Riley of Amherst was the first Black Nova Scotian to play in the National Hockey League? He was with the Washington Capitals from 1974 to 1979.

Boxing

- During the 1960s, Les Sprague of Amherst was a Canadian Boxing Federation light welterweight champion.
- In 1947 Austin Brown of Joggins won the Maritime Middleweight Boxing Championship.

Austin Brown (centre) of Joggins receives the Maritime middleweight boxing gold medal from Moncton mayor J. E. Murphy as assistant trainer Eric Gibbons looks on, November 1947

Row Your Boat

Elijah Ross of Parrsboro (1846–1920) rowed with the St. John Crew from 1863 to 1876. The group was later dubbed "the Paris Crew" after becoming rowing champions of the world at the Paris Exhibition of 1867.

Law and Order

Royal Canadian

The RCMP was established in Amherst on April 1, 1932. It serves 1,456 square kilometres (910 square miles).

Attention! Cumberland County Cadets

Army Cadets

Unit 1859 Springhill

Unit 2553 Oxford

1442 River Hebert

272 NS Highlanders

Air Cadets

689 Handley Page Parrsboro

154 Amherst Anson Amherst

Sea Cadets

258 Amherst

First in Cumberland County First in Nova Scotia

Long-distance runner Noel Paul, born in Halfway River in 1904, was the first Mi'kmaq to be elected to the Nova Scotia Sports Hall of Fame.

Government

In the 1700s in Cumberland Township, elections lasted 3 weeks and were conducted by the high sheriff.

Do You Remember?

Ash Piles

People would dump the remains from their wood and coal fires onto a designated place in the yard—usually out of the way of the front of the house. These ashes would accumulate over time into mounds. Ashes would be used for banking a house (see below), for covering over muddy and wet spots in lanes during the spring, or for covering icy patches in the winter.

Auction 45

A card game still popular in Cumberland County. The 5 and jack are the high cards of any suit that is "trump." The ace of hearts is wild. Players make bids on the first hand. In some games it's agreed that the first person or team to get to 125 points is the winner, while in others the individual(s) with the highest score after an agreed upon number of "hands" are played wins the game. There seems to be a different set of rules depending upon where in the county the game is being played. The 1990s Canadian-produced television program, *Black Harbour*, set in Nova Scotia, had its characters attend an Auction 45 card game in one episode.

Bankings

Before many Cumberland County homes had basements, a banking would be placed around them before winter. Beach stones, dirt, and ash were commonly used for this purpose. A. Murray Kinloch describes a banking as "an early form of insulation…consist[ing] of rough boards held in place by stakes, the space between the boards and the house filled with earth." He contends that the word "banking" originated with English settlers.

Being Laid Out

A dead person lying in her coffin is said to be "laid out." Years ago many of the deceased were laid out at home instead of in a funeral parlour, and neighbours and friends would visit the home to pay their respects. This custom lasted into the late 1960s in Cumberland County.

Christmas Clubs

A social group (usually of women) that would meet once a month to chat, play cards, and save money for Christmas. Such a group was started in Joggins in 1948 and still meets today. A treasurer was appointed to collect money each month and deposit it in a bank account set up for the purpose. In November or December, each woman could withdraw her portion of the money from the account to buy Christmas presents and food for the holidays. Some of the money would also go towards a Christmas meal for the group.

Coal Piles

Back when coal was burned in stoves and furnaces, coal deliveries were usually dumped in the backyard until the owners could get it shovelled away into the coal shed. Not everyone had a shed to keep their coal dry, though, and coal piles were a common sight around people's homes. "Go play in the coal pile" became a common expression spoken to someone who was bothering you.

Line of Clothes

When someone has laundry on the clothesline they are said to "have a line out" or "have a line of clothes out."

Party Lines

A party line was a phone exchange to which all phones—or a number of them—in the community were connected. One could not make a phone call if other people were already on the line. To let neighbours know the line was free (in the days of the crank phone), the caller would "ring off"—that is, turn the crank slightly to cause a short ring.

UI Stamps

Unemployed workers received one Unemployment Insurance "stamp" for each week they worked. A certain number of "stamps" meant the worker could receive Unemployment Insurance, so much the better if it was during the winter months. "Will you get enough stamps?" was often the question asked when someone reported that they had recently found a job.

Look What We've Got: Cumberland County Collections

When asked about the most interesting objects in their collections, directors, managers, and curators of Cumberland County's heritage institutions had this to say:

Ken Adams, director/curator, Fundy Geological Museum, Parrsboro:

> For me, it's the fossils in our collection. Reflecting a diversity of plant and animal life, from literally a half billion years of the earth's history, they help record and tell stories about changes in environment, Nova Scotia's paleogeography, colliding continents, shallow seas, and coal swamps. The development of terrestrial life forms, as recorded by the fossilized tetrapods from Blue Beach-Horton Bluff, Joggins, Brule, Carr's Brook, and Wasson Bluff, can be followed though the gradual transition from fish to amphibians,

then reptiles. During the Permian and Triassic periods, further diversification is recorded by the appearance of fossils from archosaurs, mammal-like reptiles, and the dinosaurs. The partial dinosaur skeletons recovered from Wasson Bluff tell their own stories of herding, migration, and life and death in the rift valley that formed as Pangea broke up. In other words, wow, the stories that these mute artifacts can tell!

Did you know...

...that Heritage Models in River Hebert recounts the history of the area with over 30 scale models of buildings and other places of interest?

SOCIETY

Sarah Welton, manager, River Hebert Heritage Models, River Hebert:

The Great Timber Raft Experiment model depicts the large cigar-shaped log raft that made its way from Two Rivers, Cumberland County, to New York City in July 1888. Lovingly crafted by Reginald "Bud" Johnson, it shows in great detail the ingenuity involved in creating this huge vessel.

Oralee O'Byrne, Curator/Manager, Age of Sail Heritage Centre and Museum, Port Greville:

Horses' snowshoes were used in many parts of the county, especially where deep snow was a concern. They were typically used on a heavy horse like a Clydesdale or Percheron. The snowshoes were made of a sturdy piece of wood approximately 30 cm x 23 cm with a series of large square bolts affixed to each end to aid in traction. Two loops of wire encircled the hoof and then a leather lace strapped the item to the foot. These shoes were commonly used in the lumber camps, maple woods, and bogs.

Jenna Boon, director, Joggins Fossil Cliff Centre:

The most interesting fossils in the collection are the fossilized bones of the earliest known reptile, *Hylonomus lyelli*, because of its significance as an evolutionary milestone, which include reptiles, dinosaurs, birds, and mammals. It marks one of the most significant events in the history of life as amniotes achieved the capacity to reproduce on land.

Susan Clarke, manager, Ottawa House By-the-Sea Museum, Parrsboro:

The most interesting artifact that the Ottawa House "By-The-Sea" Museum owns is the building itself. This 1765 hand-hewed structure is unique in many ways. It is one of the oldest known buildings in Nova Scotia today and is the only structure left standing from the mid-1700s shipbuilding and lumbering community of Partridge Island Settlement. It was once owned by our 6th prime minister, Sir Charles Tupper, in the 1870s. He named it Ottawa House.

Bronwen Forward, patron service assistant, Cumberland County Museum and Archives, Amherst:

A particularly interesting object in our collection is the player piano, which was made at the Amherst Piano Factory (in business from 1913 to 1928) and bears the name Cremonatone Cumberland Amherst & Toronto. The player piano is one of the many fine products made in Amherst during the early 1900s, a time when the town was one of the most important export centres in the Maritimes. It is still in working condition, and tourists of all ages enjoy hearing the classic songs on this impressive product of Amherst's past.

Helen Sims, office administrator, Minudie Heritage Association:

Our most interesting item would probably be the nineteen-foot section of an original Acadian aboiteau that was found by the department of natural resources on the Minudie Marsh in May 1989. We believe this may be the largest section of an aboiteau in one piece in the whole province. When the Acadians settled in 1672, Minudie was an island. This aboiteau would have been part of their drainage system and you can still see where the one-way gate would have been. This gate allowed fresh water to run off the marsh at low tide but prevented salt water flowing onto the land at high tide.

David Dewar, curator and manager, Wallace and Area Museum:

In 2006 the museum asked visitors to vote for the most interesting artifacts in the collection. Their number one choice was the book of letters written by Thomas Davison (circa 1774–1825), a shopkeeper, lumberman, and father of James B. Davison, the builder of the house that is today the museum. In total there are 265 letters in the collection, all handwritten by Davison. Over half are business letters and some are advertisements for his lumber venture. Between 1810 and 1814, he kept a copy of every business letter he wrote. Indeed, it was a common practice at the time to keep copies or first drafts of all letters written. A number of them are personal messages Davison wrote to friends and acquaintances. To fully enjoy the content of these beautiful letters, a reader needs to know their context, local slang, and nineteenth-century rules of grammar. To date the museum has transcribed about 100 of Thomas Davison's letters and plans to complete another 50 transcriptions by 2009.

Judy Jollymore, manager, River Hebert Miners' Museum:

One item that receives a lot of comments from visitors is our miners' memorial wall, which contains photographs and stories about individual miners from the area. The stories are the result of personal interviews conducted approximately 20 years ago. The miners all enjoyed telling their stories. Many of them have passed on, but their photos and words will always be here to remind us who they were. I don't think one of the men interviewed ever said they didn't like mining. In fact, during the interviews, many told me that they would go back down tomorrow if the mine was still running. They called themselves brothers.

Anne Newman, executive director, Anne Murray Centre, Springhill:

All that glitters is gold—at least it is at the Anne Murray Centre. The centre is a tribute to the legendary singer's amazing career, but it isn't until one walks into the awards room that the full scope of her accomplishments really becomes obvious. Rows of gold and platinum albums and glittering trophies of all shapes and sizes fill every inch of the room. It's breathtaking even to those who've been in the room before, but for those who haven't, it's like walking into a fantasy—a spectacular visual you'll remember long after you've left the centre.

A Poem and a Song

Reverend John Warner of Parrsboro stated that the following poem was written by his mother, who lived in Pugwash in the 1870s and was familiar with the accidental shooting of a young boy in the area.

Mind How You Trifle With a Gun

It was April on the fourteenth day
I pray attend to what I say
A gun was herd in solm sound
Like thunder roaring through the ground.

The People hastened to the spot
Whear they herd the mornful shot
oer yonder stood a man and gun
Who he the curset action don

I just went out in carless fun
On porpes for to snap my gun
When this young lad with corage bold
Run up the hil and met the load

I did not know the lad was in
Until I saw him drop his chin
A dreadful sight and sad to tel
He turned from me and down he fel

Now take young Daniel from his gor
And place him on the cortroom flor
And send for justis very soon
And let the jury fill the room

Now take young Daniel from my sight
Up with his friend to spend one night
With wringing hands and bitter cryes
They walk the floor with streaming eyes
The parent of this murdered boy
Now giving up all hopes of joy
To think their son a man not grown
Should die while in his youthfull Bloom

There is one thing i'd have you do
Lode this same gun and shoot me to
I wish to God that I was dead
Where shall I hide my shamefull head

Come all young men thats brisk and gay
I pray attend to what I say
Think on the fate of McKlerns son
Mind how you trifel with a gun

—From *Sea Songs and Ballads from Nineteenth-Century Nova Scotia*, edited by Edith Fowke.

SOCIETY

Amherst held a special Old Home Week on July 15–16, 1910, to celebrate the town and bring former Amherst residents back for a visit. Dances and receptions were held. There was a "night shirt" parade at midnight. Veterans of the Boer War and those summoned to turn back the Fenian raids did re-enactments. A concert was held by the Old Home Minstrels in the Amherst Auditorium. One song on the program was "The Amherst Girl," sung by a Mr. Thompson:

I liked the girls at Joggins,
At Oxford, thought them fine,
They were immense at Parrsboro,
At Pugwash were divine,
They all looked good at Springhill,
But my heart was set a-whirl,
And I lost it quite completely,
To the dear old Amherst Girl.

Amherst Old Home Week Parade, July 1910

Ghosts, Legends, and Tall Tales

Spooky Spectres

Muddy Ghosts

In 1754, five Acadians drowned while trying to cross the Missiquash River from French to English territory. When the river is at high tide, their ghosts sometimes appear along its banks.

Friendly Ghosts

In the late nineteenth century, rumours circulated that a peddler had been murdered somewhere between Lynn and Southampton. For years afterwards a man was often seen standing in the woods in the area and waving at passing cars.

Restless Ghosts

Around 1880, a man named Bill Eagles disappeared on Westchester Mountain. He was searched for but never found. Soon afterward, people began to report seeing a ghost on the Halifax Road, always in the same spot. One evening, Hugh Scott was coming home over the mountain on horseback. Hugh eased his horse down to a walk in order to cut himself a chew of tobacco when he noticed a man walking alongside. Recognizing Bill Eagles, who appeared to be a ghost, Hugh was frightened and whipped his horse into a run.

The next time Hugh saw his brother William, he told him about Eagles. William said that if he ever got the chance he would speak to the ghost and ask what he wanted. Several months later, William got his wish. He was travelling the mountain to Hugh's house when, his horse at a walk, he saw Eagles alongside. He said, "Hello, Bill, what do you want?"

The ghost answered, "I want to be buried."

William asked, "How will I find you?"

Eagles said, "Just a short way up this little brook under a pile of old brush." William promised to attend to the burial the next day and continued on his way.

The next morning, William and a friend went up the mountain. They found the pile of old brush, gathered up Eagles' bones, carried them out, and buried them. The Westchester Mountain ghost was never seen again.

Many years afterwards, an old man called Shacksteed was lying on his deathbed at Springhill. He confessed to killing Eagles and taking his boots. People in Westchester remembered Eagles having new boots shortly before he went missing. No sign of them had been found with his remains.

Headless Ghosts

Nova Scotia folklorist Helen Creighton collected ghost stories, a number of which took place in Cumberland County. Captain Hatfield told her of his experience with the ghosts of a headless dog. "Hatfield and one of his shipmates were on their way home from a sea trip. They were six or seven miles from Port Greville at a place known as the Ghost Hollow and they had been warned not to pass it after dark. They had an old team-horse and a lash and, when they were about two-thirds of the way up Mill Hill, a big white dog appeared at his side. The horse just stopped as if it had come to anchor but I wasn't frightened. I sang out, 'look at that dog' and jumped off the [wagon] and took the lash and struck the dog, and the lash went right through [it] as if [it]wasn't there. The dog went under the wagon and disappeared. The man who was with me was scared to death. I was a lad of fifteen or sixteen then and I often went over that same place afterwards, but I never saw it again."

Crying Ghosts

At Black's Point, near Parrsboro, is Maiden's Cave. Its name is supposedly derived from a 1750s incident when a British ship was captured by pirates near the area. All on board except, of course, the captain's beautiful daughter, were made to walk the plank. The pirates were unable to control the uncooperative young woman, and after landing at Black's Point they decided to abandon her there. They placed her in a cave and sealed the entrance with a large stone, essentially burying her alive. After hearing cries from inside the cave, some Mi'kmaq ventured near to investigate and removed the stone. They found only skeletal remains. The story goes that this poor woman still cries for help from her stony prison.

In 1877, sixteen-year-old Mary Harney of Rockley was sent out to gather up the family cows for milking. She was never seen again. Foul play was suspected in her disappearance but no one was ever charged with her murder. It is said that, on some evenings in the community, the crying of a young girl can be heard along a nearby river.

The Great Amherst Mystery

Cumberland County's best-known ghost story and poltergeist event surrounded Ester Cox, a young woman who lived in Amherst in the 1870s. Sixteen-year-old Ester had been living a seemingly quiet and ordinary life with her sisters, Jennie and Olive, and brother-in-law

David Teed, on Princess Street in Amherst. One evening in September 1878, the family was awakened by strange noises coming from the bedroom shared by Ester and Jennie. Rumblings seemed to come from under the bed and the coverings were flung off by invisible means. The family was frightened by these unexplained events. As the weeks went by, the occurrences became more numerous and deadly. Sometimes lit matches would fall from the ceiling and knives and heavy objects would fly through the air. One night, the words "Ester Cox, you are mine to kill" were etched into the wall of the bedroom.

Ester and the family were at their wit's end with these events and the publicity they were attracting. The noise from the house could be heard along Princess Street and crowds waited in the front yard for the next event. Sometimes the Amherst police needed to be called in to keep order among the crowd. The story was picked up by the media and was soon an international phenomenon. Ester would sometimes leave home and stay elsewhere to give her family a rest from the turmoil. The ghosts (there were at least two) did not appear to follow Ester to these new locations or to her workplace, a local saloon.

Over time, Ester and the family began to converse with the ghosts through a series of knocks. The number of knocks would answer a question. The ghosts now visible, but only to Ester, were an old man, Bob, and a young woman, Maggie.

American actor and opportunist, Walter Hubbell, a self-professed "painful investigator of the supermundane," heard about Ester Cox and her "ghosts" during a stopover in Halifax and wanted to investigate. He appears initially to have wanted to expose Ester as a hoax, but after living with the family for a few weeks in early 1879 he was convinced that they were victims of some malevolent force.

Hubbell thought that some good—financial good that is—might come out of letting people see Ester in the flesh after hearing so much about her. He used his knowledge as an itinerant actor to place Ester and himself on the travel circuit. She would sit on the stage while Hubbell presented a lecture. Of course the audience was there to see something happen, but it never did.

On June 19, 1879, the *Moncton Daily News* voiced its opinion of the tour: "In the name of humanity, propriety, religion, and decency, we earnestly protest against a proceeding so base and disgusting. If the girl is sick, why should her infirmities be exhibited to the public? The civil authorities ought to interfere."

Soon after, in Chatham, New Brunswick, Ester and Hubbell were chased down the street by hecklers who threw stones at them. After that the tour was cancelled.

The poltergeists continued to plague Ester for a number of years. She was once jailed, charged with burning down a neighbour's barn. She eventually moved to the United States, where she married and had children. The ghosts seem not to have followed her there. Ester Cox died in 1911.

No clear explanation of what happened to Ester Cox has ever been given. It has been suggested that she had been sexually assaulted, the trauma of which caused her to hallucinate. She was also described as "a human battery" or a "force field" that attracted supernatural energy. Whatever the explanation, the Great Amherst Mystery has never been solved.

Land and Sea Mysteries

Deadly Waters

While Champlain had named Isle Haute for its physical appearance, early Acadians referred to the island as Île aux Morts, Island of the Dead, since it seemed to trap and wreck vessels on the incoming high tide no matter what side of the channel was selected to navigate it.

Ahoy Matey!

Some of Cumberland County's stories relating to buried treasure involve pirates...

In June 1952 American author and treasure seeker Edward Rowe Snow travelled to Isle Haute on the trail of the notorious pirate,

Edward "Ned" Low (c.1690–1724), who is remembered by history as particularly cruel and depraved. Isle Haute was believed to be one of the far-flung locations along the eastern seaboard where Low buried his stolen loot.

Snow was not the only one to search for Low's treasure on Isle Haute, but he has, so far, been the most successful. He found human remains and a number of eighteenth-century gold and silver coins minted in Spain and Portugal.

...and some don't...

The 1755 Expulsion of the Acadians has been the backdrop for a number of stories of treasure in Cumberland County. As the Acadians fled to escape deportation, they are believed to have buried gold coins, church wealth, and other valuables in the area surrounding their homes or along the paths they used. The fields and forests on the Isthmus of Chignecto and in Minudie and River Hebert are believed to contain treasure. Author W. R. Bird stated in the 1920s that it was an open secret that Acadian wealth was buried on the Fort Cumberland Ridge. In Minudie, a farmer ploughing a field is said to have unearthed an iron pot filled with gold in 1845.

Mystery Ship

The most famous Cumberland County ship was the *Amazon*, a brigantine of 198 tons built in 1860 by Joshua Dewis of Spencer's Island and registered at Parrsboro a year later. It was not as the *Amazon,* however, that the ship became so well known. In 1867 the vessel was wrecked off Cape Breton, then salvaged and sold. In 1868 it was transferred to American ownership, registered at New York, and renamed *Mary Celeste*. Four years later, in 1872, the *Mary Celeste* became the most famous mystery ship of all time when it was found, deserted by captain and crew, drifting off the Azores. The reason that all hands abandoned ship has never been confirmed.

Great Balls of Fire

Reports of sightings of circular dancing balls of fire on the Tantramar Marsh go back hundreds of years. "Balls of fire" are mentioned in Mi'kmaq legends, and an Acadian story dating from the 1750s relates them to star-crossed lovers who became separated during the Expulsion. A sighting from the 1970s described the phenomenon as a series of "round balls of light circling around." Some believe they are UFOs. Historian Bill Hamilton says that "perhaps the most convincing explanation is that the 'balls of fire' are caused by the spontaneous combustion of gases from decaying marsh grass and vegetable matter. The result is a flame-like phosphorescence that flits over marshy ground."

Did you know...

...that in some parts of Cumberland County the "crust man" was the equivalent of the boogie man? If children would not eat the crusts of their bread, they were told that "the crust man will get you."

Blazing Circles

In 1991 a 10-metre-wide crop circle was discovered in a grassy field at Fort Lawrence. A compass needle was said to spin outside the ring but was unaffected inside it.

Cumberland's Witches

Placing the name of "witch" upon a person, usually an older woman, was often the result of not understanding or tolerating the behaviour of that individual. Women who were accused of being witches were often widows with little means of support, financial or otherwise. Sometimes they were free-spirited individuals who simply led eccentric lives in a conservative community.

The Witch of Inky Dell

Sir Justice Sandford of Windsor, Nova Scotia, was one of the many fictional characters created by Nova Scotia author Thomas Chandler Haliburton (1796–1865). Sandford, nicknamed "the old Judge," was a great storyteller and entertained listeners with tales of his travels around Nova Scotia. "The Witch of Inky Dell" is one such story. Haliburton often disguised the locations about which he wrote, but Inky Dell appears to be a forested valley located somewhere near the Nova Scotia–New Brunswick border.

Watch That Broom!

It was believed that if, while sweeping the floor, one person "swept around" another, the latter would never get married. In the 1940s, a young girl in Lower Cove was cautioned by a female visitor, "Don't sweep around me. I'll never get married." She never was.

The story takes place in the late 1780s and concerns a Loyalist, Captain Walter Tygart. The captain and his cronies (a young Sandford among them) frequented an area tavern to drink, tell stories, and discuss politics. The captain was known for his violent temper, and quarrelled frequently with anyone who crossed him. A common target of his anger and threats was his neighbour, the widow Nelly Edwards. Nelly, like the captain, was bad tempered and "her language coarse and violent." Her unsocial behaviour, along with her knowledge of plants and herbs, and her selling of charms and telling of fortunes, turned some people against her and they began to refer to her as a witch.

The captain claimed that Nelly was squatting on his land, and he often threatened to evict her. Soon there was bad blood between them. Shortly after they had a major row, people noticed that the captain began to act strangely. He would no longer visit the tavern; in fact, he would not leave his home after dark at all, and in the daytime he would carry a Bible in one coat pocket and a prayer book in the other. People heard him mumble to himself on occasion that his tongue was frostbitten from the cold, that he had been shut in a stable and not given oats. He also complained that he had been "kicked on the leg by a black mare." Soon, he did not leave his home at all.

One day, the area experienced an incredible thunderstorm with heavy rain and high winds. The storm caused a forest fire that devastated Inky Dell, killed Nelly Edwards, and destroyed her home.

The tavern patrons had no sooner heard the news that the Witch of Inky Dell was dead, when the captain himself came through the door claiming that he had been bewitched by Nelly Edwards and her death meant that he was again a free man. He then relayed a strange tale to Sandford and others in which he described often meeting Nelly Edwards on his way home from the tavern. He explained that they would argue and he would often end up being changed into a horse. Nelly would climb upon his back and ride furiously across the Tantramar Marsh to Fort Lawrence. The captain told his audience that when he and Nelly got to the marsh they were joined by "three other old women on black horses." When the group got to Fort Lawrence, "the old women dismounted and put us in the chaplain's stable, and left us until it was near dawn, when back they came in great haste, jabbering and muttering in some unknown tongue, took us into the yard, jumped into their seats, and off like lightning the way they came. At the place where we all met we all separated again."

The captain said that this happened a number of times over the months until, at last, he could not handle the physical abuse of being whipped and bridled, and the mental anguish of this happening to him. The only way to stop Nelly from bewitching him was to stay at home, which he did until the forest fire freed him from the Witch of Inky Dell.

The Devil Made Her Do It

In another story from *Bluenose Ghosts*, Helen Creighton tells of a girl and the devil. It was likely a cautionary tale meant to be a warning for young people interested in pursuing pleasure activities.

Creighton's informant was a child when she heard the story and remembered it as taking place somewhere between Parrsboro and

Diligent River. "Many years ago a girl was to be taken to a dance but, at the last moment, the young man cancelled. She loved dancing and, in her disappointment and distress, she said petulantly, 'I'd go with anybody who would take me. I'd even go with the devil if he came.'

"Very shortly after this a fancy rig drove up and a charming, dashing young man got out and came to the house and invited her to go to the party. She was delighted. What an impression she would make, not only upon the boy who rejected her, but upon the whole gathering. She accepted readily, thinking of nothing but this fortunate turn of events."

"The evening went off happily and she enjoyed her handsome light-footed partner. But shortly after she came home the whole house was startled by a noise like thunder. It seemed to centre around the girl's room to which she had just retired. The family rushed in to investigate and found her lying dead upon her bed. Upon her forehead was the devil's mark, the imprint of a horse's hoof. They looked up then and saw a great hole torn in the roof and recalled her rash statement when she had said she would go to the dance with anybody, even the devil. It was presumed he had answered her challenge and then had exacted his price; that he had come for her soul and had taken it with him through the great rent in the roof."

Act of God

"The community was shocked by the deaths of two young people within a week of each other, both seemingly in good health. In each case, an inquest was held by Dr. Ayre, Coroner, and the verdict was: 'Died by Visitation by God.'" — *Chignecto Post*, January 20, 1887

Economy and Industry

Just the Facts Ma'am

According to the Cumberland Regional Economic Development Association website, the five biggest employers in Cumberland County in 2006 were:

* The Chignecto Centre Regional School Board, with 850 employees
* The Cumberland Health Authority, with 650 employees
* Oxford Frozen Foods, with 350 regular employees and 550 employees during harvest time
* Correctional Services Canada at Springhill, with 350 employees
* The Teletech Call Centre in Amherst, with 300 employees

In 2001 the average household income in Cumberland County was $39,832.

A Taste of Cumberland

Mmmmmmmmaple!

Aboriginals discovered maple syrup accidentally when sap was used, instead of water, to boil some meat. It proved to be delicious of course, and the rest, as they say, is history.

A Load of Wood

One must have 1,000 tapped maple trees to be considered a commercial producer of maple products.

I'm Lovin' it

In 1982 the first McDonald's restaurant in Cumberland County opened in Amherst.

Did you know...

...that Cumberland County is the main maple syrup producing area in Nova Scotia with more than 76% of the province's taps?

Want Blueberry Maple Chocolates?

They're only available from the Appleton Chocolates Company in Wentworth.

A blueberry field in Parrsboro

On the Hoof

The first provincial exhibition was held in Amherst on July 4, 1884. Its aim was to improve livestock.

Farming by Experiment

The Nappan Experimental Farm began operation in 1887. It was one of four regional experimental farms set up across the country to assist Canadian farmers in modernizing their practices. During World War I prisoners of war from the Amherst internment camp worked at the farm, helping to bring in the harvest and perform other duties.

First in Cumberland County First in Nova Scotia

Nova Scotia's first steam-powered grist mill began operation in 1843 in Minudie.

Did you know...

...that a live bee colony can be viewed at the Wild Blueberry and Maple Centre in Oxford?

...that Oxford produces more blueberries per capita than any other community in the world, and that Oxford Frozen Foods Limited is the largest producer of wild blueberries in the world?

Rocks and Stones

Copper City

The Crown Copper Hotel in Wentworth housed employees of the copper mines.

Did you know...

...that Joggins was the location of the first underwater coal mine in Canada?

...that the Cochrane Mine in River Hebert was the last unmechanized thin-seamed coal mine to operate in the province? It ceased production in 1980.

Labour Unrest

On September 27, 1879, the first Provincial Workmen's Association, a legalized trade union, was formed in Springhill by coal miners in response to poor working conditions.

In 1919, 3,000 workers were involved in the Amherst General Strike, which lasted three weeks.

Old Coal

By 1759 areas of Joggins were being mined for coal. Coal has been mined in River Hebert since the 1830s. Commercial mining began in Springhill in 1849.

First in Cumberland County First in the British Empire

The Malagash Salt Mine was the first rock salt mine in the British Empire. The first shaft was sunk on July 1, 1918. Salt from Malagash was shipped to Newfoundland (for preserving fish) and to Toronto (to salt roadways). It produced 70,000 tonnes of salt annually and closed in 1959.

Worth Our Salt

The Canadian Salt Mine Co. Ltd. in Pugwash produces approximately 1,200,000 tonnes of salt per year. It is the only salt mine in Nova Scotia and the largest underground mine in the Atlantic Provinces.

Now That's Deep!

In 1958 the Springhill No. 2, at 4,304 feet, was the deepest coal mine in the world. By then it was the only operating mine in Springhill and had been mined continuously since 1873.

Quarry Me This

During the nineteenth century, Lower Cove, Minudie, and Ragged Reef were the three locations in the county where sandstone was quarried for the creation of grindstones. In 1847, 33,075 grindstones were shipped from Cumberland County wharves.

Work site at Lower Cove Stone Quarries, date unknown

Did you know...

...that Jim Barkhouse constructed Cumberland County's first cement block building, the Riverside Garage in River Hebert in the late 1930s?

Seaworthy

Gone Fishin'

In the Cumberland Basin, where the tides rise to a height of thirty feet, nets are strung along stakes of up to twelve feet. A ladder is required to retrieve the fish, which get caught in the netting. This method of fishing was developed by the Mi'kmaq and is still practiced in some areas of Cumberland County today. Fishermen visit their nets each day at low tide, no matter what time of day or night.

Lobster Fishing Ports in Cumberland County:

East Wallace

Gulf Shore

Malagash Point

Malagash

Pugwash Point

Pugwash

Port Phillip

Port Howe

Tidnish

Wallace

Largest in Cumberland County Largest in Canada

Seagull Pewter of Pugwash is the largest manufacturer of pewter in the country.

Industry and the Store Next Door

We Were Busy

In 1912, "Busy Amherst" was in the middle of an industrial expansion that would almost double the town's size during the first decade of the twentieth century. Its central location on the Intercolonial Railway line meant that manufacturing facilities enjoyed competitive shipping rates.

The Cars

The McKay Car, manufactured at the Nova Scotia Carriage and Motor Car Company in Amherst, was sold at dealerships in Halifax, Montreal, Toronto, and Calgary.

And the Planes

During World War II, the Canada Car Plant in Amherst built the fuselages for 1,000 redesigned twin-engine A. V. Roe aircraft known as the Anson. The planes were also flight tested in Amherst.

Did you know...

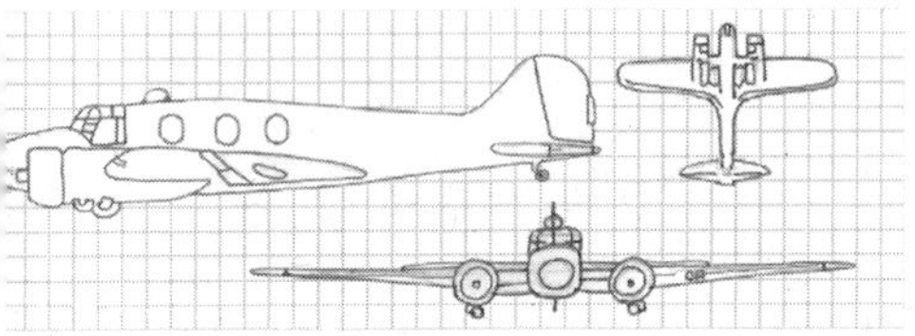

...that artist Roberta Taylor was the only female draughtswoman to work at the Canada Car plant during World War II? She designed components for the Anson airplane.

The Big House

The Springhill Institution is a federally funded medium-security prison.

Lookin' Good

Mansour's Men's Wear of Amherst has been in business since 1924.

Look Out Below

In 1998 Ski Wentworth opened the first and only snow tubing park in Atlantic Canada.

Oldest in Cumberland County Oldest in Canada

Tingley Monuments Limited of Amherst, established in 1846, is the oldest monument manufacturing company in Canada.

Here's to You

Jost Winery, winner of 150 international awards, became a licensed winery in 1983. Its first cellar was built in 1985. It is located in Malagash on the 45th parallel, the same as the Bordeaux regions of France. It is the oldest and largest continuously working winery in Nova Scotia and the only winery in Cumberland County.

Jost Winery in Malagash

Let's Get Industrial

Town of Amherst Industrial Park = 509.82 acres

Town of Oxford Development Lands = 95.53 acres

Town of Springhill Geothermal Industrial Park = 52.2 acres

Town of Parrsboro Industrial Park = 30 acres

Oldest in Cumberland County Oldest in Canada

In 1843, brothers Nathan and Charles Tupper established the first pharmacy in Amherst and one of the first in Nova Scotia. Today, Pugsley's Pharmacy is located on the site of the Tupper Pharmacy, the oldest continuous location for a pharmacy in Canada.

Play It Again

The Amherst Piano Company Limited was in operation between 1913 and 1928. According to local historian John Mackay, with the exception of "the cabinets and case portions of the pianos, they were assembled using parts purchased from piano supply companies, and ironwork cast from their own patterns in local foundries. The finished product, which included some player pianos, was called the Amherst Piano. They were constructed from local wood, with pilasters and legs, as well as bench legs, being hand-carved by a master wood carver who personally selected the local woods that were used."

Did you know...

...that the fluted columns on the Dominion Public Building in Amherst were handcarved from solid stone?

...that Wallace sandstone is included in the Peace Tower in Ottawa and in public buildings in New York's Central Park, Boston, and San Francisco?

A Place to Dock Yer Boat

Home Harbours

* Parrsboro Harbour, on the north shore of the Minas Basin, is fed by three freshwater sources: Farrell River, Mill Creek, and Whitehall Creek. The channel depth is 24 feet.
* Parrsboro became a ship's port of registry in 1850.
* Pugwash Wharf has a channel depth of 17 feet at low tide. The marine facilities in Pugwash are closed during the winter due to ice in the Northumberland Strait.

Did you know...

...that up until 1900 the Greville Bay region was the third-largest registration port for ships in Nova Scotia and was second only to the Port of Halifax for freight tonnages shipped from the province?

...that more than 700 ships were launched from the Greville Bay region?

Here We Go Again

The idea of moving ships across the Isthmus of Chignecto in order to shorten the sailing distance around Nova Scotia was first suggested by a governor of New France during the reign of Louis XIV (1643–1715).

In 1823 New Brunswick sent a representative to Halifax to discuss the project of a canal from Chignecto to Baie Verte. But in 1888 George C. Ketchum of Fredericton had another idea. He suggested a ship's railway in which large docks would be installed with hoisting machinery that would lift ships of up to 4,500 tonnes and place them on tracks that would carry them across the isthmus. At the other end the same type of machinery would lower the vessel to the water again. Ketchum proposed that the railway would run from Tidnish to Fort Lawrence, and it almost did until time and money ran out. The Chignecto Marine Transport Railway was never completed and Ketchum's dream never realized.

An artist's representation of a sailing vessel being transported by the Chignecto Ship Railway, c.1890

ECONOMY

We've Got Energy

They're Number One

Ropak Can Am Ltd. was the first industrial site in Canada to demonstrate the economic and technical viability of geothermal energy.

First in Cumberland County First in Canada

The *Amherst Gazette* was the first newspaper office in Canada to use electricity.

Good Ideas

Dr. Dara Cochrane (1893–1964), a River Hebert family physician, was a champion of economic development in the area. He established sawmills, lumber camps, and coal mines, and assisted in the development of sheep farming. He was also instrumental in establishing the River Hebert District High School.

C-Vision and its sister company, **LED Roadway Lighting Ltd. of Amherst,** have conducted research and development on what the company says is the world's greenest street lighting system. In 2009 it announced a number of test sites for the product across North America and the Middle East. Compared to a 100W high-pressure sodium street light, the new LED products could reduce energy use by 46 per cent. The LED street lights could also reduce greenhouse gas emissions by 440,000 tons over 20 years, equivalent to taking 4,434 cars off the road each year.

First in Cumberland County First in North America

Senator Hance Logan (d.1944), from Amherst Point, consulted with inventor Thomas Edison regarding the transporting of power by wire from a coal mine to a factory. Logan persuaded his co-directors of the Maritime Coal, Railway and Power Company Ltd. to build a power plant at the Chignecto Coal Mine to produce electricity. By 1906, Logan's plan was a success and he received a telegram of congratulation from Edison, "on the inauguration of the first power plant of the American continent for the generation of electricity at the mouth of the coal mine and the distribution of that power to other centres."

Power to the People

The Maccan Power plant opened on July 31, 1907, on Harrison Lake, and was dismantled in 1994.

First in Cumberland County First in the World

The first mine in the world that was flooded to produce thermal energy was in Springhill. Ralph Ross was one of the first people in Canada to explore and harness the energy from warm water below the Earth's surface.

Timber!

Cumberland County to the Big Apple

Shulie residents claim that half of New York City was built on pilings shipped from that village's wharfs. There was a demand for large timber, often in excess of 65 feet in length, for New York's growing dock area. Pilings were used for wharfs and jetties, warehouses, and sheds. Such timbers were also needed to make staging for shipbuilding.

Big Deal

By the mid-nineteenth century various Nova Scotia counties had become well known for their specific wood products. Cumberland County was famous for its deal, boards of fir or pine sawn to a standard length.

We've Got Your Lumber

Spruce and pine logs 80 and 90 feet long, 3 feet at the butt and 1 foot at the top, were not uncommon in Cumberland County.

Historic Events

Making Waves

What historian John McKay calls the "Great Timber Raft Experiment" was played out in Two Rivers, Cumberland County. Two Rivers, a community that no longer exists today, was in the 1880s, the home of lumber baron and businessman B. B. Barnhill.

The need for Canadian timber in the United States led to a search for ways to get it to markets in New York and Boston quickly and cheaply. Carrying huge logs on ships was cumbersome and tariffs were high. Hugh R. Robertson of Saint John thought he had come up with an answer—a log raft. Robertson envisioned a huge cigar-shaped raft of logs, held together with chains, and towed down the Eastern Seaboard. He was granted patents for his idea in Canada, the U.S., and abroad. Barnhill agreed to build the construction cradle and slipways for the raft.

Work began in 1885, but it would take almost three years and a number of attempts before a log raft was towed successfully into New York Harbour. On July 26, 1888, the *Halifax Morning Chronicle* reported that "The timber ship is successfully launched. Spectators cheer thunderously as the 11,000-ton monster glides gracefully to the sea at Two Rivers, Cumberland County."

During the forenoon a steady stream of carriages kept pouring in, and the raft was pretty thoroughly inspected by at least a thousand persons. At noon preparations were made for the launching. This work was overseen by an expert sent from New York by the owner. A few pieces of timber were cut away and then the fate of the raft depended upon a few strokes of a ram amidships, where the shoring was so arranged that it was only necessary to knock out a single piece.

Following the first two strokes the raft started. The descent down that ways was gradual, but not rapid. When it struck the water the raft kept its head up and skimmed along gracefully. The speed decreased perceptibly as the last 200 feet left the slipway.

An artist's representation of the triumphal arrival of the log raft in New York Harbour, August 1888

Clouds of smoke caused by the tremendous friction almost obscured the rear half of the raft from view, but soon cleared off in the breeze. The impetus of the moving monster sent it more than its length offshore. It was a grand sight. The large crowd cheered themselves hoarse as the raft glided so beautifully off the slipways. Two of the employees, Harding Parsons and Jack Carter, held their places atop the raft as it was launched and did not even get a wetting.

New York City appears to have been just as excited to witness the arrival of the towed "cigar" raft. On August 18 the *Halifax Morning*

Chronicle reported that "throngs of people flocked to the waterfront to view the huge raft. It being the Sabbath, the docks were closed with entry being provided by a single wicket. Two young boys posted themselves at the dock entrance and had charged five cents admission, collecting as many nickels as they could carry before being chased away."

The raft that made it successfully to the Big Apple was 598 feet long, 52 feet wide, and 35 feet high, tapering to 10 feet at the ends. Its weight made it, at the time, the second heaviest structure ever launched.

First in Cumberland County First in Canada

On the evening of October 14, 1869, the home of Cornelius Crowley of Streets Ridge was engulfed by fire. Mary Elizabeth, age 11, was awakened by her mother's screams. She quickly assisted her brother Gus to jump out the upstairs window to safety below and then dropped her sister Catherine into her family's arms.Tragically, Mary and Catherine died within 24 hours.

In 1870, the Nova Scotia Legislature unanimously approved a special motion to erect a monument in Pugwash at Mary Elizabeth's gravesite to commemorate her unselfish act of bravery. It was the first public monument erected in Canada to the memory of a heroine.

In Memoriam

Mary Elizabeth Crowley
lies beneath this sod, a victim
of fraternal love,
having rescued a younger
brother and sister
from the flames of her father's
dwelling.
She explained, Mother, all is
over with me now
but I have saved my brother
and sister.
She expired twenty four hours
after.
October 16, aged 11 years
Greater love no man hath
known
R.I.P.

Mining Disasters

In total, 424 men and boys lost their lives in accidents, explosions, and "bumps" in the Springhill coal mines.

The White Miner memorial has overlooked Springhill's Main Street since 1894 when it was unveiled by Governor General and Lady Aberdeen and the Right Honourable John Thompson, prime minister of Canada. It was erected in memory of the 125 boys and men who lost their lives in the 1891 explosion in the Springhill Mine. The memorial is located in Miners' Memorial Park, which also contains tablets and monuments to honour those who died in the 1956 and 1958 mining disasters.

Danny James Popular and Eric Earl McIssac, both of River Hebert, died in the Westray Mine methane explosion in Plymouth, Pictou County, on May 9, 1992.

First in Cumberland County First in Canada

Canada's first war memorial, or cenotaph, is located at Nash's Corner in Nappan. The community raised funds for the memorial immediately after World War I and it was in place for the first Armistice Day service held on November 11, 1919.

The Summer of the Handley-Page

A Handley-Page V/1500 bi-plane was on its way from Harbour Grace, Newfoundland, to New York City when it crash-landed on the Parrsboro racetrack on July 5, 1919. The plane's original mission was to compete in the race to complete the first non-stop transatlantic flight from east to west. While in Newfoundland, however, they received orders to fly to New York. Engine trouble forced a landing in Parrsboro, and repairs ensuing from the crash took three months to complete. Continuing on its journey on October 9th, the ill-fated plane ran into more trouble and bad weather forced it to land short of its destination at Greenport, Long Island. Due to the landing there, Parrsboro and Greenport became sister towns. The plane made such a big impression on the people of Parrsboro that the summer of 1919 is still referred to as the "summer of the Handley-Page."

The Handley-Page that crashed in Parrsboro on July 5, 1919

On the Beach

During the nineteenth and early twentieth centuries, with so many ships and boats going to and from harbours all over Nova Scotia, incidents of people falling overboard, drowning, and their bodies being washed ashore were not uncommon. Alec Burbine tells the story of his older brother and a friend walking the Lower Cove Beach, about 1913, when they spied a shoe on the beach and a little further along, they found the body of a man. Village authorities laid the body out in an old building near the beach and made enquiries. The identity of the man was never discovered and he was buried in a nearby cemetery.

On Christmas Eve, 2001, Tobi Gabriel of Toronto died when the car she was driving plunged off a 30-metre cliff in Lower Cove. Her three-year-old son Gage was strapped in a car seat in the back. Tobi was killed on impact as the car hit the beach, rolled over twice, and landed on its top. Early on Christmas morning, local resident Linda Belliveau was standing in her yard when she thought she heard a child crying. She followed the sound to investigate and found Tobi's body in the water and little Gage beside the car. He was fine except for frostbite and bruises. Gage later stated that "he saw two women in white dresses standing in the water smiling at him all night."

Outlaws of Nature

The Saxby Gale of October 4–5, 1869, was perhaps the worse storm ever experienced by Cumberland County. The gale, a category 2 hurricane with winds clocked at up to 165 kilometres per hour, tracked across the Bay of Fundy region, devastating parts of Maine, New Brunswick, and Nova Scotia.

Almost a year earlier, Lieutenant S. M. Saxby, an amateur astronomer serving in the Royal Navy, wrote a letter to all major London newspapers suggesting that there would be a storm of immense and devastating force on October 4th and 5th, 1869. At the time, Saxby's prediction was widely publicized; however, most people dismissed his warning. It was widely believed that no one could predict such an event nearly a year in advance. Saxby was not able to say where the storm would be located, only that it would occur:

> At 7 AM on Oct. 5th, 1869, the moon will be at the part of her orbit which is nearest to the earth. Her attraction will, therefore, be at its maximum force. At noon on the same day, the moon will be at the earth's equator, a circumstance which never occurs without marked atmospheric disturbance. At 2 PM on the same day, lines drawn from the earth's centre would cut the sun and moon in the same arc of Ascension. The moon's attraction and the sun's attraction will therefore be acting in the same direction. In other words, the new moon will be at the earth's equator when in perigee, [the point in its orbit when it's nearest to the earth] and nothing more threatening, can, I say, occur without miracle.

The *Amherst Gazette* reported: "A tremendous tide swept over the whole of the marshes of Westmorland and Cumberland…At half past ten o'clock the dykes overflowed. The waters having gradually accumulated on the marsh…a wave similar to the tidal bore, swept up with a roaring noise and great velocity, carrying almost everything before it; stacks of hay, fences, and in many cases well filled barns." A storm surge, basically a dome of water, broke through the dykes on the

Tantramar and Minudie marshes, flooding the area, drowning people and livestock, and destroying homes and property.

I Felt the Earth Move

On November 18, 1929, at 4:38 PM, an earthquake shook Cumberland County. It lasted about 20 seconds, during which time buildings swayed and dishes and windows rattled. Tremors were felt in Nappan, Springhill Junction, and Parrsboro. Springhill residents thought it was an explosion at one of the mines.

That Was No Lady

Hurricane Edna left behind a path of destruction in North America from North Carolina to the Atlantic Provinces in September 1954. In Cumberland County roofs were blown off barns and homes lost windows. Edna's winds were measured at up to 195 kilometres per hour.

POWs

During World War I a number of prisoner of war internment camps were created across the country. An inland location and good rail connections were two important elements considered in determining where an internment camp would be situated. The old iron foundry on Park Street in Amherst served the purpose in both regards. The Amherst internment camp of World War I was the largest prisoner of war camp in Canada, and at one time held more than 850 prisoners.

The foundry's main building was about a quarter of a mile in length and 1,000 feet wide. It housed the prisoners' sleeping and living quarters and, along with an exercise compound, was surrounded by barbed wire.

One morning during World War I, Adelaide (Davis) Smith of Lower Cove went out to do her barn chores. There she found a young German soldier hiding. Though unable to speak each other's language, Adelaide brought him into the house and fed him, and he then went on his way. He had likely travelled from Amherst by stowing away on the train that passed near Adelaide's home.

During its operation, twelve prisoners escaped from the Amherst Internment Camp, six of whom were never recaptured. The young man in the Smith barn may have been one of them.

German prisoners of war staged musicals and plays while incarcerated in Amherst during World War I.

Demon Liquor

Ever heard of the Big Parrsboro–Amherst–Port Elgin liquor heist of 1924? The port of Parrsboro received a lot of liquor, legal and otherwise, by boat. It was often stored at the Parrsboro Custom House until transported elsewhere.

Writer and local historian Dan Soucoup relates:

> In the early hours of November 20, 1924, as many as thirty Amherst men in numerous motor vehicles, including a hearse from the town's funeral parlour, arrived in Parrsboro and parked outside Customs House. Their plan included knocking out the alarm system and phone. But after the robbers entered the building and were loading

the whiskey and rum into their vehicles, a single alarm tipped off the town that something was amiss. Customs officer Henderson and town Police Chief Smith were notified and came to investigate. A daring cops and robbers chase ensued through the back roads of Cumberland County.

— "Big Fundy Shore Booze Raid," *Looking Back: From the Pages of the Times & Transcript*, p. 230.

The usual modus operandi of Amherst and area bootleggers was to make it across the border into New Brunswick, where Cumberland County authorities couldn't chase after them. When the coast was clear they would drive back over into the county. On that November day in 1924, some of the culprits made a clean getaway. Others didn't.

We Are the World!

The Joggins Fossil Cliffs became famous in 1851 with discoveries there by geologists Sir Charles Lyell and Sir William Dawson. The cliffs are discussed in Charles Darwin's groundbreaking 1859 work, *On the Origin of Species.*

The Joggins Fossil Cliffs were designated as a UNESCO World Heritage Site on July 7, 2008. This designation was the result of much planning and dedicated work by a number of groups and individuals over many years.

The cliffs' 14 kilometres of coastline are regarded as the world's best record of life in the Carboniferous Period (coal age) of 300 million years ago.

The Joggins Fossil Cliff Centre was opened to the public in May 2008. The $9 million, 13,000-square foot interpretive centre includes a gift shop, lab, and exhibit space. The mission of the Joggins Fossil Institute, which manages the beach in Joggins, is to "hold for the benefit and education of humanity a collection and a geographic site representative of the Carboniferous Period and ensure that the site and collection is conserved and safely studied and exhibited. The Joggins Fossil Cliffs provide engaging visitor experiences that inspire wonder and build an understanding of the natural world."

Joggins Fossil Cliffs Centre

Aged Like Fine Wine

Jost Winery celebrated the designation of the Joggins Fossil Cliffs as a UNESCO World Heritage Site by placing images of fossils on the labels of two of their award-winning wines: 2006 Marechal Foch and 2007 L'Acadie Chardonnay.

Let There Be Light...

Cumberland County still has working lighthouses at Apple River, Parrsboro, Cape d'Or, Cape Sharp, Cold Spring Head, and Wallace. Some ports formerly represented by lighthouses are now served by small, automated electric lamps installed by the Coast Guard.

...along the Glooscap Trail

Apple River has been home to three lighthouses. The first was built in 1848 and the second in 1870. Neither is standing today. The third was built about 1965 and its light was automated in 1973.

The **Cape d'Or lighthouse** was built in 1922. Today it is part of the Fundy Shore Ecotour and is the only lighthouse in the province where visitors can stay overnight. The light was automated in 1995.

Built in 1886 at the entrance of the Parrsboro Harbour, the **Cape Sharp lighthouse** was automated in 1989.

There have been two **Parrsboro lighthouses**. The first was built on Partridge Island on the west side of the mouth of Parrsboro Harbour. The second one was built in 1980 and became automated in 1987. It is located on a bar at the west side of the harbour entrance.

When the **Port Greville lighthouse** was built in 1908, it was lit with kerosene oil. No longer used by the early 1980s, the building was cut in two and shipped off to the Coast Guard College in Sydney, Nova Scotia. It was brought home again in 1998 and today has a new life, not far from its original location, as the Age of Sail Museum.

The **Spencer's Island lighthouse** was built in 1904 and ceased operations in 1988. It was opened to the public in 1991 as a museum, and in 1995 was designated as a municipal heritage site.

...along the Sunrise Trail

The **Cold Spring Head lighthouse**, located on Route 366, was built in 1890 and automated in 1980.

The **Pugwash lighthouse**, long known as the Fishing Point Lighthouse, was built in 1871. Originally located at the east side of the harbour entrance, it was replaced by a tower in 1961.

There were two **Mullins Point Range Lights** in Wallace Harbour. The first was built in 1873, the second in 1894. The former is standing but no longer operational; the latter no longer exists.

The **Wallace Harbour Range Lights** are located on the northeast extremity of McFarlane Point. The lights were automated in 1993 and one is still operational.

Did you know...

...that the Amos Seaman School Museum is the oldest remaining one-room schoolhouse in Nova Scotia?

Cold-Blooded

In about 1837, in the River Philip area, a farmhand with the last name of Doyle murdered farmer Clem Stanley and attempted to murder Stanley's housekeeper and her daughter. Fortunately the latter two both survived and were able to identify the culprit. After the murder, Doyle appears to have calmly helped himself to a snack of cake and bread from the Stanley kitchen; authorities reported bloody fingerprints in a tub of butter. Doyle then walked from River Philip to Amherst Head and hired someone to drive him to Dorchester. Authorities caught up with him in Memramcook and brought him back to Amherst. He was later found guilty, hanged, and buried in Minudie. People there were afraid of Doyle and at one point a village priest had the remains dug up so it could be confirmed that the murderer was still in his coffin.

The Last Hangings in Cumberland County

What was described at the time as "the most brutal murder ever committed in the Maritime Provinces" occurred in Amherst on February 3, 1933, when 18-year-olds Alvah Rufus Henwood and Trueman Mortimer Smith entered the Croft Street home of Mabel Smith and murdered her. Mrs. Smith was bludgeoned by a baseball bat and her throat was cut. The culprits got away with $130. Mrs. Smith's body was later found by her 17-year-old son. Henwood and Smith were arrested two weeks later, supposedly just after Henwood got married. The men had been under suspicion early in the investigation, as they had left lots of evidence behind them. Their fingerprints were found on a number of objects, including a cash box and light bulbs. In addition, Henwood had been spending money and couldn't explain how he had earned it.

From the start, the object of the crime was theft. Henwood confessed that he had been prepared to rob the Smiths a week before, but had lost his nerve and decided that he needed assistance. He turned to his childhood friend Trueman Smith.

The two young men were hanged in Amherst on September 12, 1933, in the last execution in Cumberland County and two of the four last such hangings in Nova Scotia.

A Cold Case

The murder of Sadie Mae Rogers, of Amherst, has never been solved. Rogers, 80 years of age, lived alone on Cordova Street. She was last seen alive on September 26, 1981.

Newsworthy

Cumberland County's three most newsworthy events of the past 20 years, according to *Citizen* editor Andrew Wagstaff:

- The construction of the Cobequid Pass highway from Amherst to Truro, and the decision to make it a toll road, created a lot of headlines in the mid-1990s. Local MP Bill Casey led an effort to remove the toll, but to no avail. It was particularly controversial because, at around the same time, money was taken from the project and diverted to the Fleur-de-lis Trail, a secondary highway that just happened to be in the riding of the transportation minister of the day. For years residents had called for the twinning of the Trans-Canada Highway through Wentworth Valley (nicknamed "Death Valley" because of its high rate of fatalities), but no one was thrilled about paying a toll to use the new road.

- The collapse of the Springhill arena's roof in 2001, during a peewee hockey game, could have been tragic if a few individuals hadn't acted quickly and got the building evacuated in time. But the real story came in the following months, when the community, known for its tragedies and hard luck, pulled together once more to rebuild a bigger and better community centre.

* The designation of the Joggins Fossil Cliffs as a UNESCO World Heritage Site in 2008 after years of preparation by local individuals and groups to put forth a successful application. The real impact of this story won't be realized for years to come, but it has already served to put a tiny, somewhat desolate, Cumberland County village on the world map.

Interesting Phrases and Expressions

With ongoing changes in transportation and communications, the generation of the early 1930s may be the last to remember, or even to use, many of the phrases and expressions that are particular to Cumberland County. The county's linguistic heritage is moulded by the backgrounds and experiences of the people who live there: Mi'kmaq, Acadians, English, Irish, Blacks, and many others.

Until the advent of electricity, television, and the automobile, which took families "to town" for shopping and supper, people in Cumberland County took evening walks, sat on the front doorstep or veranda, and conversed with neighbours. Community interaction was a lifeline for people of all ages. Children learned what to say and how to say it by listening to their parents and grandparents. Today, the children of Cumberland County learn from TV, the Internet, and their iPods.

The phrases and expressions recorded here are but a sampling. Though often funny and insightful, many are unkind and used to ridicule. They all reflect the verbal inventiveness of people struggling to survive in a harsh environment, whether social or physical. They are a window into both the past and the present of Cumberland County.

Able

Used to describe a man who had performed a feat of strength: "Mr. Man I want you to know he was some able." Probably from the nautical term "able-bodied seaman."

Aboard

To attack someone either physically or verbally: "I went aboard her."

An' 'em

Corruption of "and them." Used in describing a group of people: "Mom an' 'em went up to Amherst this morning."

Arse/Ass

- Arse/ass over kettle (to fall down): "He was walkin' when all of a sudden he went arse over kettle."
- "Got the world by the arse on a down-hill pull" describes someone with an easy life.
- Burnt your arse: "You burnt your arse, now you have to sit on the blisters." Same meaning as: "You made your bed, now lie in it."
- Tear your arse. To be upset and act out: "She'll be tearing her arse about that now."
- Drag yer arse/ass. Describing someone who is slow: "We'd get to town if Laurie could drag her arse out of bed." Can also be a command to do something: "Drag yer arse an' get those dishes done!" Or a command to just leave: "Drag!"

Back to

Someone with their back turned: "I couldn't see him because he was back to" or "Back to, you'd think she was her mother."

Bag a [of] nerves

Used to describe a nervous person: "She's just a bag a nerves." Pronounced as "bug a nerves" by a Scottish woman in River Hebert whose expression caught on over time.

Big-feeling

To be proud or boastful: "He always was big-feelin'."

Big people (adults)

"There was a time for the big people last night."

Blow

To describe someone who brags or is boastful: "He's always blowing about something."

Boston States

The New England states: "He's gone to the Boston States." Many residents of Cumberland County emigrated to Boston and surrounding areas in the late 1800s and early 1900s to find work.

Bunch a hairs

Someone who has a lot of hair or just a bad haircut: "There's bunch a hairs goin'." Can also refer to a person in general.

Bunting against me

Pronounced "buntin' agin me." Someone is bothering you or getting on your nerves: "She was buntin' agin me at the school meeting last week."

By Gee, don't be sayin'

An oath, meaning "Is that right?" Said with a shake of the head and/or a look of amazement on the face; probably a corruption of "By Jesus."

Chew the rag

To complain: "They were all in there chewing the rag," "All she does is chew the rag," or "No wonder I chew the rag all the time." Dan Soucoup cites "ragging on it," having a slightly different connotation in New Brunswick to describe someone who "will not give up and keeps bringing it up when no one wants to hear about it." May have been derived from the practice of providing a moist rag to teething children to relieve their sore gums.

The clear rig

The right tool for the job: "That's the clear rig for getting a car out of the ditch" or "This coat is the clear rig for winter."

Clear sheer

Used for emphasis: "He is a clear-sheer idiot."

Cold

"As cold as the north end of a moose yard."

Come

Used in prophesying the future: "Come a big storm we won't be ready" or "Come winter you'll be glad to have that jam."

Come rate back around

To recuperate: "He was on death's doorstep and he came rate (right) back around."

Couldn't

- Describing an incompetent driver: "Couldn't drive a cat downstairs with a broom."
- Describing an incompetent carpenter: "Couldn't nail a button on a shithouse door."
- Describing a bad singer: "Couldn't carry a tune in a bucket."
- Describing a bad cook: "Couldn't parboil shit for an owl."
- Describing a person, family, or group who lack money: "Couldn't make a down payment on a sucker."

Cow or can?

Question asked of someone who wants milk in their tea. Cows' milk is homogenized, while "can" referred to the ever-present Carnation Milk container.

Cramp

Said of an annoying situation: "Wouldn't that just cramp ya?" or "Wouldn't that cramp your grandmother?"

Crick

A mispronunciation of the word creek: "He lived at Mill Crick all his life." Can also be used as in "I got a bad crick in my neck."

Crooked

Said of a person considered dishonest: "Crooked as a dog's hind leg."

Cross-eyed

"She was so cross-eyed that when she cried the tears ran down the back of her neck."

Crow

Telling someone that you got out of bed early: "I was up at the crack of crow's piss." Also used to describe a bragging person: "That one is always crowing about something."

Dead

A child who looks or acts like his parent or other relative: "His father will never be dead as long as he's alive" or "He's the dead image of his father."

Devil

A dragonfly: "Devil's darning needle." Sometimes shortened to "Devil's darn needle."

Dirty

To be in a bad mood, frustrated, or upset: "He was some dirty after that happened" or "He was right dirty the other night."

Dog

Meaning one must be tough to survive in this world: "It takes a big dog for a hard road." Other expressions: "She's so homely/mean/loud she'd scare a dog from a gut wagon" or "He's so homely he'd scare a dog from her pups."

Doin's

The responsibility or organization of something: "He's got the doin's of that."

Don't

- "Don't let me hear a peep out of you." Be quiet, stop talking.
- Don't let on. A warning not to acknowledge that you know what happened or is going to happen: "Don't let on you see her."

* “Don’t you lend a mind to no one.” Advising someone not to pay any attention to what others may say, think, or do.

Drunk

Used as a noun, it means a party: “There was a big drunk on at Ian’s last week.”

Dull

When a knife or any other blade needed sharpening it was said to be “Dull as a hoe.”

Dustin’

* Said to describe someone moving quickly, usually a child: “Did you see Elizabeth?” “Yeah, she was there dustin’ around.”
* Can also describe someone driving fast: “He went dustin’ through Amherst.”

Euchred

To be done for, to be dying: “Is she very sick?” “Oh, she’s euchred.” The expression comes from the card game euchre, which is popular in both Europe and North America.

Eyes

Said of someone who had a “dirty look”: “She gave me a pair of eyes—let me tell you.”

Face longer than a wet Sunday

Used to describe someone looking sad or upset.

Face tied in a knot

Used to describe someone in a bad mood who is looking angry or sad.

Fass

A mispronunciation of fast—to be stuck or caught: “Don’t go in there or you’ll get fass.”

Fetched up

To hit or run into something and be stopped short: "He fetched up when he hit the ditch, let me tell you."

Fill your boots

Go ahead, do whatever you want, take all you want: "Can I have some cake?" "Go ahead—fill your boots."

Flour

"You'll have to eat a lot more flour to be as strong as me." Said to a person smaller or physically weaker than you.

Fly

Either being sent to your room or told to hurry up in doing something: as in "Fly up those stairs" or "Fly the Jesus up those stairs."

Fly into

To attack someone either physically or verbally: "I'll fly into her the next time I see her" or "She flew into him—don't think she didn't."

Foolish

* Crazy or misinformed, used a lot as "Don't talk so foolish" or "Don't be so foolish" or "He's right foolish."
* Can also be used to blame a parent for a spoiled or unmannered child: "She made a total fool out of that one."

Frig

May chiefly be used as a polite alternative to other curse words: "Frig off" or "What the frig is he up to?"

From away

A term used to describe someone not originally from the area or county: "She's from away."

Full to the gunnels

A corruption of the word "gunwales"—a part of a ship. When something is full to capacity or someone has eaten a lot they are said to be "full to the gunnels."

Git steppin'

Meaning to get a move on or hurry up: "Rachel better git steppin' if she wants to go to bingo tonight."

Giving

Used in reference to the weather report on the radio or TV: "What did they give for the weather tomorrow?" or "What does the weather give?"

God love ya/her/ him

Praising someone: "He works hard, God love him" or "God love ya, you've had a hard life."

Goin' town

"Are you goin' town after work?"

Got

Often pronounced as "gut."

Got 'er made

To be prosperous, to have good luck: "He's gut 'er made ever since his mother left him all that money."

Grease-fittings

Said of a talkative person: "She must have grease-fittings on her jaws."

Guv

To give, or gave: "I guv it to him."

Half bubble off plum

Describing someone considered a fool: "He always was half bubble off plum."

Handcuffed

When someone asks you to do something they could easily do themselves, you in turn ask them: "What's wrong with you—you handcuffed or something?"

Hand-running

Pronounced "han-runnin'." Meaning that something happened over and over: "Two days han-runnin' he was late for work."

Hang crepe

To complain or be very negative: "All he ever does is hang crepe." In reference to the funerary practice of hanging black cloth around the house after a death in the family or community. The person doing the complaining is called "a crepe hanger."

Happy

* Said in an emphatic response to someone who you agree with or who agrees with you: "You're happy right it's cold out."
* Also used in the expression "The only way I could be happier is if there was two of me."

Hard-lookin' ticket

Someone who is drunk, homely, or not well-dressed: "He's a real hard-lookin' ticket this morning."

Hard shape

"Bob's in hard shape since his accident." Can also be used to described someone who is hungover.

Harmless

Said of someone considered to be friendly or shy: "It's only Gordon—he's harmless."

Harping

To keep talking or complaining about something over and over: "Is he still harping on that after all this time?" or "Don't start harping about that again."

Have a feed

To eat a lot of food: "I had a big feed of smelts last night." Also known as a scoff: "We cooked a big scoff last night." Usually referring to seasonal food like lobster or clams.

Head

* "He's got more than lice in his head." Said of someone considered intelligent.
* Advising someone to not be so foolish: "Give your head a shake and come out of it."

Head out

To leave: "I'm heading out for home now" or "He headed out two hours ago."

Heist

A fall off something; to fall from a great height: "Watch out—you'll give yourself a heist off that thing."

Hell

Describing something that is frozen or won't be moved: "Hard as the hubs of hell." Can also describe the opposite: "Hot as the hubs of hell."

Hills

Climb the stairs to bed: "Go up the wooden hills."

Home

The place where one has grown up. No matter how long one has lived in another province or country they are always asked something like "When did you get home?" or "How long are you home for?"

Homely

Someone who is ugly: "She's homelier than two people" or "He's so homely he could gag a maggot."

Horse

Said of someone known for telling falsehoods: "He lies faster than a horse can trot."

Hot/hotter

To be overheated from working hard: "Hotter than a hen hauling wood."

I'd

* To read someone the riot act; to set them straight: "I'd be tellin' him right off."
* Said of an arrogant or boastful person: "I'd like to buy him for what he's worth and sell him for what he thinks he's worth."

Imagine

A number of meanings depending upon the inflection of the voice. Can mean incredulity: "Allan left today—imagine." Can mean agreement on something: "It's raining hard." "I imagine!" Or can mean agreeing to do something (if only half-heartedly): "Can you drive me to River Hebert?" "Oh, I imagine." Often pronounced as "magine."

Into "him" for

To owe someone money: "I'm into him for a hundred dollars" or "She's into me for twenty bucks."

It

Used as a pronoun instead of she or he in reference to a person: "What did it want?" or "Here it comes now." Likely developed from the translation of pronouns from French to English.

Jack

To "jack" game (hunt with a light at night). The flashlight blinds the animal, which is rendered motionless and therefore easy to kill: "That one is always jacking deer."

Jag

A large load of hay or wood: "He had a big jag of wood on his truck when I saw him." Also a drunken spree: "I had a real jag on last night."

Jimmy White

Said to someone who has a toe sticking out of a hole in their sock: "Jimmy White's out of jail."

Jump

To be emphatic about something, as in: "to jump up and down." I often heard it expressed in the negative as a warning not to be so sure of something: "I wouldn't jump up and down and say that."

Keep on

Meaning to persist, often used in a negative sense: "You'll be sorry if you keep on" or "He kept on until he got sick."

Land

Used as a verb, it means to arrive or come for a visit: "Somebody always lands here at mealtime" or "Who was that that just landed in the yard?"

Last

Telling someone that this is the last time, that they won't be doing a particular activity—such as shopping or going for a car ride—again. Usually said to a misbehaving child: "Make this your last."

Let on

To pretend or make believe: "Let's let on that we're mad at her."

Light for out, lit out

To leave: "He lighted for out at six o'clock" or "He lit for out at six this morning."

Light Into

To attack someone verbally or physically: "She's going to light into him when he gets home."

Live

"I wouldn't live there if they gave it to me." Said of an unsuitable house, town, or province.

Long-headed

Said of someone who is smart or well organized: "He's some long-headed."

Look at the head on that

To ridicule someone's hair or hairstyle: "Look at the head on that walking down the road."

Looks like a scared peep

Phrase used to describe someone timid or shy: "She looks like a scared peep."

Louse

Said of a stingy person: "He's so tight he'd skin a louse for its tallow."

Lucifee

When I was growing up I'd hear things like "That one's got a head like a lucifee," meaning someone had messy or unkempt hair. Also heard, "You look like lucifee." During my father's childhood (late 1930s to late 1940s), he heard people say to unruly children: "Stop that or the lucifee will get you." I had always thought that it was a corruption of the word Lucifer; however, according to A. Murray Kinloch the word originated with the English Loyalist settlers who corrupted the Acadian word for lynx: *le loup cervier* to *lou'cerfies* or lucifee.

Make on

To pretend or make believe: "Make on that we are running away."

Mister man

Used for emphasis: "Mister man I want you to know that it's some cold out."

Mouth

Said of someone who is talkative or loud: "He's got a mouth on him."

Nerves

Said of a nervous or anxious person (usually a self-description): "Ain't got a nerve left."

Never make old bones

Said of someone who is thought not to live much longer: "She'll never make old bones."

Never said

To describe someone who neglected to acknowledge you: "I saw that one in the Co-op and he never said hello, good-bye, kiss my arse, or nuthin'."

No bigger than

Used to describe a child or small person: "She's no bigger than a fart in a mitten" or "He's no bigger than a minute."

Not doin' a thing

Usually said to describe the lack of care someone is receiving from a doctor or while in the hospital: "They're not doin' a thing in here for the poor soul."

Old

When describing someone who is very old: "He's as old as a man and a boy."

On the/his/her way out

Meaning one is close to death: "He went to the hospital last week; he's likely on his way out."

On the stick

To be up early and on time: "You'd better be on the stick tomorrow morning."

Out and out

Likening one person to another either for their looks or actions: "He's his old man out and out."

Peddling news

Someone who gossips: "She was over here last night peddlin' news."

Peeling

To attack someone verbally or physically, to "beat them up" or "tell them off" (i.e. "to give someone a peeling").

Pesogue

Gaelic for face. Pronounced in some parts of Cumberland County as "vasogue," perhaps as a mispronunciation of the word but with the same meaning: "Look at the vasogue on that!" I always assumed that "vasogue" was a mispronunciation of *visage*, the French word for face; however, it may be a combination of French and Gaelic.

Picture

"Take a picture, it'll last longer." You say this to someone who you think has been staring at you.

Pigs

* The backside of an overweight person is said to look like "two pigs fighting in a sack."
* Said of someone smoking a cigarette: "She looks like a pig with a straw stuck in its arse."
* Said of a messy housekeeper: "Couldn't keep house for two pigs."

Plate

* Said to a person with a lot of food on their plate. "You'll need sideboards on that plate."
* Describing something flat: "Flatter than piss on a plate." I have also heard this used in a violent context: "I knocked him flatter than piss on the plate."

Got herself pregnant

Usually said of a young unmarried woman: "She went and got herself pregnant." A physically impossible task, to say the least.

Pritnear

Pretty near, or very close. "He pritnear killed himself with that car."

Puttin' on

To show off, act out, to display emotions as at a funeral or wedding: "That one was sure puttin' on at Alton's wedding last week."

Rate

A mispronunciation of the word "right." Used for emphasis: "He was rate mad at her."

Put it rate to the boards

To drive fast.

Run with

To run/run with is to be having an affair: "He run with her for years until his wife caught them."

Running the roads

Meaning never home, and usually said of a woman: "All she does is run the roads."

Set

"I was set." Meaning that you only needed one number to be called and you would have won the bingo game.

Set to

A verbal and/or physical argument or fight: "Reg and Gordon had a set to last night."

Shake a cold

Dr. Ram Boodoosingh said that he had never heard that one needs to "shake a cold" except in River Hebert.

Shit through a goose

To have diarrhea: "Those berries went through her like shit through a goose."

Shit to a blanket

Said of someone who follows another around: "She stuck to me like shit to a blanket."

Short

- "She's so short she's going to sue the government for building the road too close to her arse."
- "She's so short she has to stand on a cigarette paper to look in a duck's ass."

Shy around

To flirt with someone or be romantically interested in them: "He's always shying around her."

Side up

To clean or straighten up a room: "I sided up the kitchen this morning." In sixteenth- and seventeenth-century Europe, tables and chairs were placed along the walls of a room, the chairs often hung from pegs. There was little furniture in the middle of the floor as there is today. This phrase may have originated from that practice. Dan Soucoup writes that it was used in New Brunswick in the context of "Let's side up," i.e. straighten up and do a light cleaning, as "Let's side up the camp before we go."

—*The New Brunswick Phrase Book: Old Sayings, Expressions, & Odd names of New Brunswick,* p. 68

Simmet

A nightdress. Barb Thompson remembers her Springhill grandfather chastising children for still being in their pyjamas in the late morning, saying to them "Why are you still in your simmet this time of day?"

Skate

A woman of loose morals: "She was a real old skate, that one."

Skiff of snow

A skiff of snow is a small amount of the white stuff: "We had just a skiff of snow over Christmas."

Skin of the nightmare

Said of someone who looks really bad or has been ill: "She looks like the skin of a nightmare."

Slewed sideways

To be dishevelled or disorganized: "He came in here with the shirt all slewed sideways" or "She was all slewed to one side when she got here."

Some

Used as an adjective for emphasis: "He was some happy to get home" or "It was some hot last week."

Spell

Used in a number of ways, usually to describe someone's mood—especially a bad one. A person who is either not talking or continuously arguing: "I went over there last night and he had a spell on." People who are in a silly mood are often told to "come out of their spell." Also used in reference to a convulsion or seizure: "He took some kind of a spell last night and had to be taken to the hospital." People who are not fond of work or just taking a day off can be said to be having "a lazy spell." Someone who is moody or acting out of the ordinary can be described as "taking a crazy spell."

Spit
"I'm so mad I could spit nails."

Spult
A chip on an enamel pot or dish: "Don't drop that pot or you'll put a spult on it."

Stand twice to cast a shadow
Describing someone who is very thin: "That Annie would have to stand twice to cast a shadow."

Storm-stayed
Stranded or kept from home because of a snowstorm: "I got storm-stayed at Beatrice's last week when it snowed so hard."

Sunday fine socks/shoes
Dress socks and shoes usually worn on Sundays either to church or to a funeral. Usually not worn through the week unless one has an office job. "He was walking out in the snow with his shoes and Sunday fine socks." Also called "Sunday fines."

Supple
Pronounced *soup-el*; meaning flexible: "Mister man he was some supple for his age."

Take boss
To take charge of something, to take over: "As soon as he got there he began to take boss" or "That one is always trying to take boss."

Take for back
To go somewhere, to leave: "It's late—I have to take for back before dark" or "He took for back two days ago."

Teeth

"Her teeth are so far apart she could eat corn through a picket fence."

Tend the house/kids

"Mum an' em went to Amherst and I had to tend the kids" or "She tended house for him for years and what thanks did she get?"

That or that one

Used as a pronoun instead of "she" or "he" in reference to a person: "What did that one want?" or "Where is that going?" Probably developed from the translation of certain pronouns from French to English.

That should

- "Well I picked up that gift for him—that should shut him up for awhile."
- Meaning she won't have to talk about that anymore: "That should keep that train whistle from blowing."

Tight

Used to describe a person who doesn't like to part with her money: "She is so tight she squeaks."

Time

An event: "They had a time for the big people last night." A time is usually held at night and alcohol is served.

Tom Pepper's dog

Someone who is slow moving was said to be "as slow as Tom Pepper's dog."

Tuning

To attack someone verbally or physically: "What she needs is a good tuning" or " I gave him a tuning up—let me tell you."

Turn around

To have to do something all over again or to do something one didn't want to do: "I went up to Amherst this morning and had to turn around and go again this afternoon."

Ugly

* Said of someone who is angry or in a bad mood: "He was some ugly when I saw him yesterday" or "She is in an ugly mood today."
* Sometimes said of a homely person: "Somebody must have beat him with an ugly stick."

Up to the States

A phrase often heard relating to travelling to the United States. Likely due to the fact that from Nova Scotia one route to the States was to drive up into northern New Brunswick to cross the border, and then drive south into the state of Maine.

Up a stump

To be pregnant: "She was up a stump and it took her nine months to get down."

Useless

Describing someone lazy or incompetent: "Useless as a five-wheel wagon."

Vassang

Name for someone who is out of control, crazy, spoiled, or undisciplined: "That kid is a real vassang." Likely a corruption of a word from one language to another.

Walk it to ya

Eat something or take some medicine. When we were kids, not feeling well and refusing our medicine, Dad used to say, "Walk it to ya, it'll make you better." This was also his response to someone who was refusing to eat or eating very little.

Well there now

Used as an expression of affirmation or mild surprise, feigned or otherwise: "Well there now, I didn't know you were coming home today."

West

Western Canada was usually described with the blanket name of "out west," which was usually pronounced "out wess."

Wide as two axe handles and a plug of chewing tobacco

Used to ridicule someone's physical size, usually the width of their behind.

Word

No word of a lie: "Listen—no word of a lie—I saw him do that."

Work

Describing someone who is not employed: "He's too heavy for light work and too light for heavy work."

Write it on ice

Said to someone who owes you money and who claims they will pay you back: "We'll write it on ice." In other words, "Forget about it."

Zeer or zear

To feel or look nauseated, disgusted, or ugly: "I felt right zeer after I ate that" or "She is right zeer looking." This is likely a corruption of a word translated from another language.

Image Sources

Barry Norris: page 12

Nova Scotia Tourism, Culture and Heritage: page 13, page 28, page 99

Cumberland County Museum and Archives: page 36 (84-57-2), page 42 (88-4-124), page 47 (82-12-2), page 48 (2004-6-5), page 78 (79-13-37B), page 93 (88-3-239), page 103 (91-99-4), page 106 (2005-01-01), page 109 (88-4-79)

Pugwash Conferences on Science and World Affairs, Washington D.C.: page 37

Anne Murray Centre: page 39

Rena Kossatz: page 60

Kay Brown: page 68

Jost Vineyards Ltd.: page 96

Archives & Special Collections, Harriet Irving Library, University of New Brunswick: page 99 (MG H 53. Series 2.6 #115)

WHW Architects, Halifax c/o Joggins Fossil Cliffs Centre: page 111

Selected Bibliography

Advocate District School. *What's Cooking in Advocate and Area?* Advocate, NS: Advocate District School, 2005.

Bird, Will R. *A Century at Chignecto: The Key to Old Acadia.* Toronto: Ryerson, 1928.

Brown, Roger David. *Historic Cumberland County South: Land of Promise.* Halifax: Nimbus, 2002.

Clarke, Ernest. *The Siege of Fort Cumberland 1776: An Episode in the American Revolution.* Montreal: McGill-Queen's University Press, 1995.

Cole, Darrell. "RCMP continue investigation of 26-year-old murder case." *Amherst Daily News,* October, 2, 2007, p. 1.

Creighton, Helen. *Bluenose Ghosts.* Halifax: Nimbus, reprint 1994.

Croft, Clary. *Celebrate! The History and Folklore of Holidays in Nova Scotia.* Halifax: Nimbus, 2002.

Cumberland Trivia 1999 Game. A Millennium Project of Heritage Models and Dr. D.M. Cochrane Memorial Medical Centre, River Hebert, Nova Scotia.

"Earthquake rocks homes and buildings." *Amherst Daily News,* November 22, 1929. Cumberland County Museum: 81-6-69b.

Fairfax, Raylene. "Blacks in Cumberland County 1600-1920." Unpublished manuscript, Cumberland County Museum.

Fowke, Edith, ed. *Sea Songs and Ballads from Nineteenth-century Nova Scotia: The William H. Smith and Fenwick Hatt Manuscripts.* New York: Folklorica, 1981.

Gautreau, Evalyn. *Shulie: The Way It Was.* Amherst, NS: Amherst Township Historical Society, 1986.

Girard, Philip, and Rebecca Veinott. "Married Women's Property Law in Nova Scotia, 1850-1910." In *Separate Spheres: Women's Worlds in the 19th-Century Maritimes,* edited by Janet Guildford and Suzanne Morton. Fredericton, NB: Acadiensis, reprint 1997.

Haliburton, Thomas Chandler. *Sam Slick.* Toronto: McClelland and Stewart, 1923.

Hamilton, William B. *Place Names of Atlantic Canada.* Toronto: University of Toronto, 1997.

Hand, Chris M. *The Siege of Fort Beauséjour.* Fredericton, NB: Goose Lane Editions/The New Brunswick Military Heritage Project, 2004.

Hubbell, Walter. *The Great Amherst Mystery.* Amherst, NS: Babineau, [1888] reprinted 1982.

Kinloch, A. Murray. "The English Language in New Brunswick 1784–1984." In *A Literary and Linguistic History of New Brunswick,* edited by Richard Guerin, Robert Whalen, and Henri-Dominique Paratte. Fredericton, NB: Goose Lane Editions, 1985.

Mastin, Catherine M., et al. *"The Talented Intruder" Wyndham Lewis in Canada, 1939–1945.* Windsor, ON: The Art Gallery of Windsor, 1993.

McCully, Helen, and Dorothy Crayder. *The Christmas Pony.* Indianapolis: Bobbs-Merrill, 1967.

McKay, John G. *Events in Local History.* Amherst, NS: John G. McKay, 2002.

———. *Gems of Amherst History Volume I and II.* Amherst, NS: John G. McKay, n.d.

Milner, W.C. "La Valliere of Chignecto." *Acadiensis* 1 (3, 1901): 157–162.

———. "La Valliere of Chignecto." *Acadiensis* 1 (4, 1901): 213–224.

Nunn, Bruce. "Ferry Story," *Lifestyle Maritimes* 7 (3, 2008): 52–53.

Poitras, Jacques. "Trotsky was prisoner in Amherst POW camp: NS town finds spot in Soviet history." *Times-Transcript* (Moncton), August 6, 1988, p. 17.

"Robbery the object of gruesome crime." *Amherst Daily News*, February 5, 1933.

Sauder, Fred. "World War II aircraft industry in Amherst." *The Citizen*, March 25, 1989.

Soucoup, Dan. *Looking Back: From the Pages of the Times & Transcript.* Halifax: Maritime Lines, 2002.

———. *The New Brunswick Phrase Book: Old Sayings, Expressions and Odd Names of New Brunswick*. Lawrencetown Beach, NS: Pottersfield, 2006.

Theriault, Mario. *Great Maritime Inventions 1833–1950*. Fredericton, NB: Goose Lane Editions, 2001.

Thurston, Harry. *Atlantic Outposts.* Lawrencetown Beach, NB: Pottersfield, 1990.

———. *Tidal Life: A Natural History of the Bay of Fundy*. Camden East, ON: Camden House, 1990.

Trotsky, Leon. *My Life: An Attempt at an Autobiography.* New York: Merit, 1970.

Tye, Diane. "The Role of Watson Weaver, Itinerant Peddler and Local Character, in His Community of Northern Nova Scotia." *Culture and Tradition* 6 (1982): 40–51.

Tye, Diane, and Peter Latta. "Symbols of Change: The Legacy of Two Early Twentieth-Century Nova Scotian Builders." *Nova Scotia Historical Review* 9 (2, 1989): 18–34.

Varkaris, Jane, and James E. Connell. *Early Canadian Timekeepers*. Toronto: Stoddart, 1993.

Selected Websites

Agriculture and Agri-Foods Canada, www.agmrc.org

Amherst, Nova Scotia, www.amherstns.com

Bill Hamilton's Tantramar Flashback, www.billhamiltonflashback.ca

Canada Trails, www.canadatrails.ca

CBC Digital Archives, http://archives.cbc.ca

Chef2Chef Culinary Portal, www.chef2chef.net

Cumberland Regional Economic Development Association, www.creda.net

Cumberland Regional Library, www.crl.library.ns.ca

Environment Canada, www.atl.ec.gc.ca

Fundy Geological Museum, www.fundygeo.museum.gov.ns.ca

Governor General of Canada, www.gg.ca

Historica, www.histori.ca

Joggins Fossil Cliffs, www.jogginsfossilcliffs.net

Maple Syrup @mmmaple, www.mmmaple.com

Multicultural Trails of Nova Scotia, www.multiculturaltrails.ca

Nova Scotia Business Journal, www.novascotiabusinessjournal.com

Nova Scotia Lighthouse Preservation Society, www.nslps.com

Nova Scotia Species at Risk, www.speciesatrisk.ca

Ottawa House By the Sea Museum, www.ottawahouse.org

Seagull Pewter, www.seagullpewter.com

Ship's Company Theatre, www.shipscompany.com

South Shore Now, www.southshorenow.ca

Springhill and Area, www.centralnovascotia.ca

The Canadian Encyclopedia, www.thecanadianencyclopedia.com

The Springhill Heritage Group, www.sybertooth.ca

Town of Oxford, www.town.oxford.ns.ca

Town of Parrsboro, www.town.Parrsboro.ns.ca

Trails Nova Scotia, www.trails.gov.ns.ca

Village of Pugwash, www.pugwashvillage.com